CHANGED *through* HIS GRACE

CHANGED *through* HIS GRACE

BRAD WILCOX

DESERET BOOK
SALT LAKE CITY, UTAH

© 2017 Bradley Ray Wilcox and Deborah G. Gunnell Wilcox Family Trust

All rights reserved. No part of this book may be reproduced in any form or by any means without permission in writing from the publisher, Deseret Book Company, at permissions@deseretbook.com or P. O. Box 30178, Salt Lake City, Utah 84130. This work is not an official publication of The Church of Jesus Christ of Latter-day Saints. The views expressed herein are the responsibility of the author and do not necessarily represent the position of the Church or of Deseret Book Company.

DESERET BOOK is a registered trademark of Deseret Book Company.

Visit us at DeseretBook.com

Library of Congress Cataloging-in-Publication Data
Names: Wilcox, Brad, author.
Title: Changed through his grace / Brad Wilcox.
Description: Salt Lake City, Utah : Deseret Book, [2017] | Includes bibliographical references.
Identifiers: LCCN 2016043270 | ISBN 9781629722863 (hardbound : alk. paper)
Subjects: LCSH: Atonement—The Church of Jesus Christ of Latter-day Saints. | Grace (Theology) | Jesus Christ—Mormon interpretations. | The Church of Jesus Christ of Latter-day Saints—Doctrines. | Mormon Church—Doctrines.
Classification: LCC BX8643.A85 W548 2017 | DDC 234—dc23
LC record available at https://lccn.loc.gov/2016043270

Printed in the United States of America
LSC Communications, Crawfordsville, IN

10 9 8 7 6

*To Matt and Natalie Burt
and a moment on the Sea of Galilee I'll never forget.
"Peace, peace, be still."
(Hymns, no. 105)*

CONTENTS

Acknowledgments ix
Introduction: The Grace He Proffers Us 1
Chapter 1: "Full of Grace and Truth" 6
Chapter 2: A Covenant Relationship 26
Chapter 3: Receiving Grace 44
Chapter 4: The Spirit: Messenger of Grace 66
Chapter 5: Escaping Bondage 89
Chapter 6: "I Know in Whom I Have Trusted" 113
Chapter 7: Succored by Grace 126
Chapter 8: Saved by Grace 142
Chapter 9: Transformed by Grace 166
Chapter 10: *Muchas Gracias* 186
Notes 199
Index 209

ACKNOWLEDGMENTS

I express appreciation to Joseph Smith, who allowed us all to more fully understand and enjoy the Lord's "grace and gifts renewed in latter days" (*Hymns*, no. 167). Like him, I, too, am a "lover of the cause of Christ."[1]

Thanks to Lisa Roper at Deseret Book who believed in this project and gave me a deadline. This book would never have been written without her consistent encouragement and help. I am indebted to my wife, Debi, and our family: Wendee and Gian Rosborough, Russell and Trish Wilcox, Whitney and Landon Laycock, and David Wilcox. How I love them! They are always my earliest and best sounding boards and editors, along with being the brightest lights in my life. Brett Sanders, who may as well be family, selflessly read early drafts and suggested important changes. His understanding of doctrine, talent

ACKNOWLEDGMENTS

as a writer, and deep love for the Savior make his feedback and friendship invaluable.

Special thanks to Tyler Rostedt and his parents, Bill and Leanne, for letting me share their story, as well as to Brent and Lori Rich, who were going through their own battle with cancer at the same time they opened their hearts and home to the Rostedts. Thanks as well to Stephen and McKenna Dutcher for permitting me to share their personal journey. I am convinced our chance meeting was not at all by chance. I also appreciate Mitch Kawai and will forever be thankful for his courage and positive choices. These wonderful friends inspire me, and I am thankful for their examples and trust.

I am grateful to Amy White, with whom I once spoke at Women's Conference on the topic of grace. I have included portions of our talk in this book. Thanks to Sheamus Kelly, Mark Richins, Spencer and Angela Olsen, Kenzie Shoemaker, Matthew C. Godfrey, Garrit Van Dyk, and Sara L. Allen. Additionally, thanks to Mallory Albrecht, Kolby Hales, Kim Hathorn, Alan Sackett, Jon Hill, Matthew Merrill, and Bret and Fiona Ostler for their doctrinal insights. As always, the team at Deseret Book has been amazing: Laurel Day, Tracy Keck, Emily Watts, Shauna Gibby, and Malina Grigg. Finally, thanks to Cody Sanders, who keeps me exercising. It is one thing to write about change and another to live it. Her support and friendship make it easier.

Introduction

THE GRACE HE PROFFERS US

"Have you been changed by grace?" This is the question I asked several years ago when I was invited to give a Brigham Young University devotional address. It became a life-changing question for Brad McNary, his wife Rachel, and their five children.

Recently, Brad wrote me this e-mail: "A couple years ago the seams that held the fabric of our family together were splitting apart. My relationship with Rachel was broken and we were losing our oldest daughter. Everywhere I turned the outlook was grim and I was terrified. I felt the bottom was about to fall out of my life." At that low point, two LDS missionaries arrived. Brad and his family began attending church. He recalled, "I had been raised as an evangelical so I appreciated how closely the LDS Church aligned with the description of Christ's Church in the

New Testament, but I worried because I didn't hear much said about grace."

Brad asked the missionaries, "Do Mormons believe in grace?" The elders assured him that we do and provided some materials to study, including that BYU devotional. Brad wrote, "Your question, 'Have you been changed by grace?' really made me consider for the first time how I was responding to God's grace. It made me think about my life and placed me on a path toward humility and repentance for major obstacles—sins that surely would have ruined our family."

The McNarys were baptized on July 26, 2014, and sealed a year later. In Brad's e-mail, he wrote, "My wife and I are closer than ever. Our oldest daughter is happier and making better choices. We are now an eternal family and serving faithfully in the Church. We have been changed through His grace."

On the cover of this book is Walter Rane's beautiful depiction of Christ healing the blind man (see John 9:1–7). I love how the painting shows this man turning toward Christ, but I love even more how Christ is reaching out toward the man. This is how the Savior reaches out to all of us.

The full extent of His reach is clearly demonstrated in the text of a favorite hymn: "I stand all amazed at the love Jesus offers me, confused at the grace that so fully he proffers me" (*Hymns*, no. 193). The word *confused* can mean perplexed and disoriented, but it can also mean overwhelmed. Indeed, we should feel overwhelmed by the magnitude of Christ's grace. *Proffers* is more than a synonym for *offers*. Adding the prefix *pro* to *offers* indicates that instead of simply extending a gift to someone, the giver takes initiative to proactively place the gift before the receiver.

Think of the emblems of the sacrament. They are not simply offered to the congregation. Latter-day Saints don't approach the front of the chapel to take them. Rather, the bread and water are proffered to us—literally placed before each of us individually, even when we are late and standing in the foyer (and don't ask me how I know that). This teaches us much about how lovingly the gift of grace is given.

Proffers *is more than a synonym for* offers. *Adding the prefix* pro *to* offers *indicates that instead of simply extending a gift to someone, the giver takes initiative to proactively place the gift before the receiver.*

Nevertheless, in Doctrine and Covenants 88:33 we read, "For what doth it profit a man if a gift is bestowed upon him, and he receive not the gift? Behold, he rejoices not in that which is given unto him, neither rejoices in him who is the giver of the gift." We stand all amazed at the grace Jesus proffers us, but He must stand a little amazed Himself at how many are unwilling to receive His selfless gift. The emblems of the sacrament simply sit in trays when we refuse to accept and internalize them.

The purpose of this book is to help all of us choose to receive Christ's grace and more fully rejoice in the gift and the Giver. Some, like Brad McNary, wrongly assume that Latter-day Saints do not believe in grace or that it does not play a central role in our doctrine. This is not so. The Restoration offers a fullness of knowledge concerning grace. Camille Fronk Olson, chair of Brigham Young University's ancient scripture department, has written, "By linking teachings and history in the New Testament and the Book of Mormon . . . we can observe multiple angles for applying the doctrine of grace and replace our perplexity with greater clarity."[1]

Many Christians turn to the Bible alone to understand this topic, but Latter-day Saints can enjoy a broader perspective. We can read Paul's teachings about grace in the context of the plan of salvation and temple worship—the very perspective with which Paul surely wrote them. The scriptures of the Restoration are full of grace. Joseph Smith's teachings are full of grace. General conference addresses are full of grace. Our hymns are full of grace. I have chosen to draw from all these sources as "we contemplate [His] lasting grace" (*Hymns*, no. 169).

We must understand what grace is, what it isn't, and its connection to the Atonement. We need to know how a covenant relationship allows us to receive grace in greater and greater abundance and escape the bondage of addictions. Through the Holy Ghost—the messenger of grace—we can be strengthened, saved, and also transformed. As we more fully value and appreciate grace, we can offer it to others as liberally as it is offered to us.

God is a "God of grace" (*Hymns*, no. 88). His gift is not a prize for the righteous. It is the source of righteousness. His help is not a reward for the worthy. It is the source of worthiness. It is not waiting for us once we change. It is the power we need throughout the entire perfecting process. No wonder we sing with all our hearts, "Oh, it is wonderful, wonderful to me!" (*Hymns*, no. 193).

Chapter 1

"FULL OF GRACE AND TRUTH"

Many Christmases ago my parents-in-law gave Debi and me a beautiful set of dishes we could use to entertain friends and family during the holiday season. This twelve-piece set has dessert plates based on the traditional carol "The Twelve Days of Christmas." The first plate has an artistic rendering of a partridge in a pear tree with the words written below. The second plate depicts two turtle doves, and so forth, up to twelve drummers drumming. One year as I set the table, I saw something on the fourth plate I had never noticed before. The words beneath the picture read, "Four colly birds." I wondered how such a glaring spelling mistake had been made. I had always heard and sung, "Four *calling* birds."

I pointed out the error to family members helping in the kitchen, thinking everyone would have a good laugh. Instead, my son said, "Dad, I think the plate's right and you're wrong."

"FULL OF GRACE AND TRUTH"

With the help of Google, we looked up *colly* and discovered it was indeed the word used in the 1780 version of the song. It was a regional English expression for "black." So, on the fourth day of Christmas the singer's true love sent four black birds! Who knew? It was not until many years later that carolers began replacing the word with *calling*. Isn't it interesting how something I thought I knew so well—something I was absolutely sure of—could change?

Calling birds. Colly birds. Who cares? Such a change is trivial. However, in many ways we can experience the same transition in our knowledge of grace, and that change is not trivial. Just when we think we comprehend it, something happens to expand and deepen our understanding. Such has been the case for me. Truly understanding grace is essential because it helps us avoid the extremes to which some have taken this doctrine. It also helps us recognize the upward pull within us and rely more fully on the merits, mercy, and grace of our Savior as we respond to that pull.

> *Truly understanding grace is essential because it helps us avoid the extremes to which some have taken this doctrine.*

MEANING OF GRACE

On the outside of Westminster Abbey in England are carved the words, "May God grant to the living, grace." Few would disagree with the plea, but for what exactly are we pleading? Like many English words, *grace* has multiple meanings. It can describe elegance and beauty or kindness and courtesy. It can be a prayer ("saying grace") or a salutation ("Grace be unto you"). In Hebrew the word means favor or goodwill given with compassion. Perhaps this is why Christians throughout the centuries have used *grace* to describe God's favor, goodwill, and love. However, grace is more than a description of God's attributes. It is how He engages with us as we strive to attain those attributes. It is the power that propels us upward toward perfection and exaltation (see Moroni 10:32). President Dieter F. Uchtdorf defined grace as "the divine assistance and endowment of strength by which we grow from the flawed and limited beings we are now into exalted beings."[1] Thus, grace is the strength He offers in order to make us strong. It is the divine help He offers in order to make us divine.

When I was younger I associated God's grace with gifts that would be mine only after I did my very best to reach the finish line. Now I realize grace applies right here and now. It is the force that gets me to the finish line. I once saw grace as an equation of my part plus God's part as if I had to meet some sort of minimum height requirement to enter heaven. Now I see it is not about height, but about growth. Elder D. Todd Christofferson taught, "We do not need to achieve some minimum level of capacity or goodness before God will help—divine aid can be ours every hour of every day, no matter where we are in the path of obedience."[2] Instead of a ratio, I now see a relationship in which "all needful grace will God bestow" (*Hymns*, no. 88). Instead of seeing Christ as making up the difference, I now see He makes all the difference.

The word *grace* probably shouldn't be used as a catchall label for every divine interaction. God grants us many tender mercies and answers to prayer. When my son Russell was finishing school to become a nurse anesthetist and was assigned a clinical rotation in a hospital four hours from where they were living, my daughter-in-law Trish was discouraged. Not only would she be caring for two toddlers on her own, but they had just had their third child, and the baby was fussy and not sleeping well. Trish didn't know how she was going to do it. When the rotation started, the baby suddenly began eating better and sleeping through the night. Our family knew we had witnessed a tender mercy.

When Russell was a teenager he lost the only set of keys for our car. He and his friend backtracked their steps and looked everywhere without success. Finally, Russell prayed and asked God to lead him to the lost keys. When he found them in a place he had already searched multiple times, our family knew we had witnessed an answer to prayer.

Such experiences touch our hearts, build our faith, and are definitely included under the large umbrella covering the many ways God reaches out to assist us. However, with President Uchtdorf's definition in mind, the word *grace* best describes the times God's assistance enables us to "progress and grow in righteousness."³ For example, when we are able to resist temptation, break bad habits, or develop patience and charity, we can see God's grace is shaping and molding our characters. When we can faithfully endure a tragedy or forgive an offense, we witness God's grace. Thus grace can be clearly evident in our lives even when tender mercies and answers to prayer are not.

Grace is different from the Atonement. It is not Christ's suffering, death, and Resurrection. Instead, grace is the power that flows from those sacred moments. Sheri Dew, former member of the Relief Society general presidency, has called it "the power the Atonement makes available to us."⁴ Long ago, people looked forward to the Atonement. Now the act of the Atonement is past. Either way, grace allows its influence to be continuous. When someone says, "The Atonement helped me," the words may be well intentioned, but they are not completely accurate. It is Jesus Christ who helps us through His Atonement. Grace is the help His Atonement makes possible.

It is Jesus Christ who helps us through His Atonement. Grace is the help His Atonement makes possible.

Grace is not priesthood in the narrow sense of authority and keys, but it is priesthood in the broader sense of God sharing His power with His children (see D&C 84:20–21). Grace is not a priesthood ordinance, but essential ordinances invite greater endowments of grace into our lives.

Grace comes from the Godhead. We can speak of receiving grace from God and Christ interchangeably (see 1 Thessalonians 1:1). Grace also comes from the Holy Ghost, "the agent of the Atonement."[5]

The Bible Dictionary states, "Grace is an enabling power" ("Grace," 697). In today's world, parents are often warned about enabling their children's bad choices by shielding them from natural consequences. Such enabling handouts become *disabling* despite the best of intentions. Grace is not a handout but a hand up. Notice how the definition in the Bible Dictionary combines the word *enabling* with the word *power*. God is not enabling us to bypass His laws but empowering us with an increased ability to live His laws. Grace is not the absence of God's high expectations. It is the presence of His power—a portion of His unlimited capacity that allows us to join with Him and do together what we could never do alone.

I once had the opportunity to speak at a young single adult conference in Kirtland, Ohio. The young people enjoyed touring the historic sites, participating in service projects, and interacting at the dance. The highlight of the weekend was a sacrament service held in the Kirtland Temple. What a moment it was for all of us to renew our covenants with Christ in the very place where Christ renewed His everlasting covenant with us in this final dispensation. As I stood to speak at that special meeting, I drew the congregation's attention to the beautiful windows and intricate woodwork on the pulpits. Then I pointed out one of the building's flaws. "Remember," I said, "this edifice was built by volunteers who knew little about construction." I mentioned some of the minor problems with construction that one of the tour guides had previously pointed out to me. Although the builders had done their very best, there were still minor flaws in the building. Nevertheless, when Christ appeared, He accepted the building as His—flaws and all (see D&C 110:7). Where there was weakness, He provided strength and transformed an imperfect building into a holy temple.

Christ will do the same for us. Our flaws and inadequacies can turn us to the Lord and force us to acknowledge our total dependence on Him. Through His grace, He can strengthen us and make us holy. Paul described grace like this: "I can do all things through Christ which strengtheneth me" (Philippians 4:13). Ammon said, "Yea, I know that I am nothing; as to my strength I am weak; therefore I will not boast of myself, but I will boast of my God, for in his strength I can do all things" (Alma 26:12).

PERILS OF GRACE

Perhaps the reason Latter-day Saints have been hesitant in the past to speak and teach about grace is that we never want to be seen as going to the same extreme as many other Christians when it comes to this doctrine. Sadly, too many in the world see grace as little more than permission to sin and procrastinate rather than the power to become "dead to sin" (Romans 6:2) and "born of God" (Mosiah 27:25). Too many live like spiritual couch potatoes and still expect God to beam them up when the time comes. They view grace as a get-out-of-jail-free card that exempts them from living even the most basic of commandments. They speak endlessly of forgiveness but rarely of repentance. They see ordinances as nonessential "works" and believe their rejection of them will be overlooked by God because "by grace are ye saved through faith" (Ephesians 2:8). Latter-day Saints agree with Christian authors who label such views as "cheap grace"[6] or "easy-believism that makes no moral demands on the lives of sinners."[7]

Sadly, this kind of thinking has led to a world in which people see little difference between the lives and choices of many Christians and those who profess no religious beliefs at all.[8] C. S. Lewis warned, "If conversion to Christianity makes no improvement in a man's outward actions . . . then I think we must suspect that his 'conversion' was largely imaginary."[9]

Kanzo Uchimura, one of the most well-known and widely

respected Christians in Japan's history, came to the same conclusion. He converted to Christianity but was disillusioned when he traveled to the United States. Missionaries had told him America was the ideal Christian civilization, where everyone celebrated Christmas and Easter, but Kanzo was totally unprepared for the swearing, dishonesty, snobbery, and prejudice he found displayed on all sides by people who claimed to be saved by the grace of the Son of God. He wrote, "If it was Christianity that made the so-called Christendom of today, let Heaven's eternal curse rest upon it!"[10]

At the same time that some Christians have gone to the extreme C. S. Lewis and Kanzo Uchimura described, some Latter-day Saints have gone to the opposite extreme. We say, "God helps those who help themselves" or "We've got to meet God halfway" and are slow to recognize our complete dependence on Christ. Too many view His grace as a final boost into celestial glory once we've gotten as far as we can on our own steam. We speak often of repentance but struggle to feel forgiven—especially when we are tempted with the same sins over and over.

Our pioneer heritage has enthroned hard work, grit, self-control, and willpower above all other virtues. We roll up our

Too many view His grace as a final boost into celestial glory once we've gotten as far as we can on our own steam.

sleeves, put our "shoulder[s] to the wheel" (*Hymns*, no. 252), and "save ourselves with all our dead" (*Hymns*, no. 5). Instead of feeling safe and confident in God's care, we never quite feel good enough. We awake early, go to bed late, read, pray, serve in callings, and still feel that we are falling short. We become so focused on checking items off our to-do lists that we forget why God gave us those lists in the first place. We read about good examples and instead of feeling inspired, we feel discouraged. Think of Mother's Day. A lot of members don't even like to go to church that day because instead of being uplifted when someone talks about his "angel mother," they feel guilty for not being better mothers or children themselves. This attitude sometimes breeds a culture of unrealistic expectations, perfectionism, and comparison that affects health and happiness.

Author Robert L. Millet calls both of these extremes "theological traps"[11] or the "perils of grace." He reminds us that in reality, faith and works are not at odds with each other: "Faith always manifests itself in faithfulness. Salvation may come by grace alone, but grace is never alone."[12]

Perhaps the answer for all of us is found within the text of the hymn "Sweet Hour of Prayer." We sing, "And since he bids me seek his face, believe his word, and trust his grace, I'll cast on him my ev'ry care" (*Hymns*, no. 142). Maybe Christian friends need to believe Christ's word a little more. When He called for disciples to keep the commandments, He meant it (see Matthew 7:21; Luke 9:23; John 14:15). Maybe Latter-day Saints need to trust Christ's grace a little more. When the Lord said, "My grace is sufficient," He meant it (see D&C 17:8; 18:31; 2 Corinthians 12:9; Ether 12:26). By avoiding perilous extremes, we can all find the desirable middle ground where we can seek His face more sincerely and cast on Him our every care more confidently.

AN UPWARD PULL

As we consider all "his grace imparts" (*Hymns*, no. 146), few can imagine a greater gift than the opportunity to be sealed together with their families for eternity. Yet, knowing the struggles all families face, perhaps the greatest gift is not only that families can be sealed, but that they can be healed so they *want* to be together forever.

When my son Russell was in the Missionary Training Center in Spain, he participated in a question-and-answer session with the teachers. All the missionaries were asked to write questions on papers, and then the instructors would pull the papers from a bowl and respond. Not too long into the session, one of the teachers fished out Russell's question and read it aloud: "What if we are teaching a family that doesn't want to be sealed for eternity?" The teacher said, "Well, that's a silly question. Who wouldn't want to be sealed forever?"

Actually, it was *not* a silly question. We spend much time

and effort in temples sealing ancestors together, but maybe they were in unhappy marriages. Perhaps some women were trapped into staying with their husbands because they were financially dependent on them. We might be sealing children to parents who were abusive. Comfort is found in understanding that vicarious work for the departed never overrides people's agency, but it is also found in knowing that people can change. If I were answering Russell's question, I would have said, "If people say they don't want to be sealed, they don't need to be. However, those desires may change as people change."

Through Christ's grace, people can change. Here and hereafter, families can change.

Through Christ's grace, people can change. Here and hereafter, families can change. We can all be helped to "overcome and avoid bad and to do and become good."[13] The Savior can change our very natures.

"Accept yourself" and "be who you are" are great slogans when it comes to physical characteristics over which we have no control. However, when it comes to moral choices that define our characters, these phrases become little more than excuses. By rejecting absolute truth and creating their own versions of right and wrong, many people seek to erase the need for change, improvement, and emulation of the divine. They speak of tolerance and acceptance but want it to extend in only their direction. They don't realize that one-sided tolerance and acceptance can quickly become vices rather than virtues as they begin to threaten freedom for everyone.

I sometimes wonder how much tolerance and acceptance Moses would receive in our modern world. What kind of reply would he get from an editor if he were to submit the Ten Commandments to a mainstream publisher today? I imagine it would read something like this:

Dear Moses:

Thank you for your submission, but it is obvious your hand is not on the pulse of what people want in our society. Are you serious about not swearing? I think that part of your manuscript should be deleted, since everyone swears. Haven't you seen a movie or walked through an airport lately? Sabbath day? That one had better be cut too, or at least revised to make church attendance optional and sports acceptable. From Little League to professional games, do you realize how much Sunday sports do for our economy? The graven image thing can stay since nobody worships idols anyway. However, I'm afraid people might realize their money and material possessions can be considered gods and then they could be offended. Safer to cut it altogether. The "don't steal" and "don't kill" bits can stay since most agree on those, but you can't mention anything about copyright laws or abortions, or the book will never sell. My biggest concern is with the section on adultery. The way you have written it sounds so old-fashioned. What if readers have chosen to have open marriages or define marriage differently than you do? This is a politically-charged issue, and you have left absolutely no room for personal interpretation, so I would prefer that you soften the language. Call pornography harmless adult entertainment and sex outside of marriage moral as long as those involved love each other. Once you make these revisions, I invite you to resubmit, but don't get your hopes up. I can't foresee this manuscript being a bestseller.

>Sincerely,
>A Concerned Editor

Although many people don't believe change is possible or even necessary, at one time or another we all reflect on our poor choices and ask, "Is this it? Is this as good as it gets?" Pop psychologists and amateur atheists would answer, "Yes! Embrace who you are!" However, deep inside we hear a different answer. We have all felt an upward pull to rise higher and be better.

President Henry B. Eyring has assured us this feeling "comes from our Heavenly Father. The opposing thought, that the upward pull is an illusion, comes from the adversary, who wants us all to be miserable, as he is." President Eyring continued, "Heavenly Father does more than allow you to feel that upward pull. He has provided a way to rise higher, almost beyond our limits of imagination, not by our own powers, . . . but through the power of the atonement of His Son, Jesus Christ."[14]

Similarly, Elder Jeffrey R. Holland testified, "Only the adversary, the enemy of us all, would try to convince us that . . . people don't really improve, that no one really progresses. And why does Lucifer give that speech? Because he knows *he* can't improve, *he* can't progress, that worlds without end *he* will never have a bright tomorrow. . . . Don't fall for that. With the gift of the Atonement of Jesus Christ and the strength of heaven to help us, we *can* improve."[15]

MERITS, MERCY, AND GRACE

In the Book of Mormon we read, "How great the importance to make these things known unto the inhabitants of the earth, that they may know that there is no flesh that can dwell in the presence of God, save it be through the merits, and mercy, and grace of the Holy Messiah" (2 Nephi 2:8). Let's examine more closely what is communicated by all three of those key words.

Christ's *merits* mean He was the only one authorized and able to perform the Atonement. His anointing in the premortal world, unique birth, and perfect life made Him the only one who could atone for us. The fact that He chose to do so means He loves us.

Christ's *mercies* mean that He was willing to save us from the physical and spiritual deaths that came in consequence of the Fall. Even though we are completely undeserving, He can resurrect us, forgive us as we repent, and enter a covenant relationship with us. The fact that He chooses to do so means He loves us just the way we are.

Christ's *grace* means that He stands ready to transform and exalt us. He offers His divine help throughout that perfecting process. The fact that He chooses to do so means He loves us enough not to leave us just the way we are.

It is this miracle of transformation that is often the focus of our prophets, seers, and revelators. A look at their general conference addresses over the last fifty years reveals that the most quoted verses from the Book of Mormon have been Mosiah 3:19 (putting off the natural man and becoming a Saint through the Atonement), 3 Nephi 27:27 (the manner of men we ought to be—even as Christ), and Moroni 10:32

Christ's grace *means that He stands ready to transform and exalt us.*

(coming unto Christ and being perfected in Him). Do you see a theme? The Brethren are consistently teaching us of both the need to change and the power to change. We don't have to settle for the status quo. We can all "triumph in redeeming grace" (*Hymns*, no. 163)

This was the message that caught the interest of my great-great-grandmother, Louisa Gwyther. She was the daughter of a wealthy Protestant minister in England. As a child, Louisa read the Bible, but she felt confused at the contradictions she saw between what Jesus taught and the religious practices that surrounded her. She felt there had to be something better. In 1849 she heard the Mormon missionaries and attended LDS church services. The members were living the way she wanted to live. She realized this was the fullness she had been waiting for. One week later, unbeknownst to her family, she was baptized in the middle of a big storm. She climbed down a rope from her second-story bedroom window and met the missionaries, who had to break the ice in a stream to baptize her. When the secret came out, Louisa was disowned and cast out of her home for joining what her parents called "that low-down set of people." She was forced to make her own living as a maid and seamstress.

Not long after this, Louisa met her husband-to-be, George Taylor, at a church meeting. She was in a silk dress and wore her dark hair in long ringlets. George told his friends that she was the girl he wanted to marry. They told him she was out of his league, but George won Louisa's love, and they were married in 1853. Two daughters soon followed. They longed to immigrate to Utah to be with the Saints but lacked sufficient funds.

George decided to move to America, where he could earn money faster and then send for his wife and family to join him.

Louisa's father heard that George had "abandoned" his daughter and her two children. He sent Louisa's sister to plead with her to denounce the Mormons and divorce her husband. Her father promised that his granddaughters would be well educated. Louisa told her sister that she valued education but had found something even more important. She had found the fullness of the gospel. She was not content to settle for less when she could have more. She wanted her daughters to have an education, but she also wanted them to know and love the Savior. Her sister departed, and soon George sent enough for Louisa and their girls to sail to America.

The voyage was difficult. Louisa and her daughters were traveling in steerage. Fearing lice, Louisa cut her and her daughters' long hair. A storm blew the ship off course, which delayed their arrival in New York by several weeks. Food was being rationed. Louisa became so ill she was confined to her bed while her two daughters roamed the deck and made do as best they could. Louisa prayed to be spared until she could deliver her girls to their father. One night a man came to her with some bread and cheese. The food lifted her spirits and gave her the nourishment she needed. From that moment her health began to improve. When the ship finally landed, Louisa asked the captain who the kind man was so she could thank him. The captain listened to her description and assured her there was no such man on board. She knew she had received divine help and strength beyond her own.

Louisa was soon reunited with George, and the family made their way west. Because of Louisa and George and other ancestors like them, I have been blessed with the restored gospel they treasured and for which they sacrificed. In Louisa's home she had learned of Christ's merits and mercies, but it was only when she encountered His grace that she was changed. Like Louisa, we don't have to settle for less. We can choose "a more excellent way" (Ether 12:11).

In 2 Nephi 2:6 we read, "Redemption cometh in and through the Holy Messiah; for he is full of grace and truth." That phrase, *grace and truth*, is important enough that it is found in all the standard works (see John 1:4; D&C 93:11; Moses 1:32). Like other words we've examined thus far, these also have great meaning—especially when they are coupled together.

Because Christ is full of truth, He saw that Louisa could become more than she was. He knew what her choices would mean to her posterity. He also sees us as we really are and as we really can be (see Jacob 4:13). He sees worth when we see worthlessness. He sees potential when we see limitations.

He sees worth when we see worthlessness. He sees potential when we see limitations.

Because Christ is full of grace, He can share His vision with us and engage with us in reaching our potential. He helped Louisa see that her life could be more meaningful than she ever dreamed, and He helped her make the needed sacrifices. The Lord is willing to do the same for us. Because Christ is full of truth, He knows the greatness written in our spiritual DNA. Because He is full of grace, He can and will unlock it as we turn to Him.

Each December our family enjoys pulling out the holiday dishes commemorating the twelve days of Christmas. Whether we sing about calling birds or colly birds, it makes little difference. However, our understanding of grace makes a big difference. It helps us avoid doctrinal extremes and, just as it did for Louisa, it helps us desire to change and draw closer to the Savior, who makes it possible. On the *real* first day of Christmas we didn't receive a partridge in a pear tree. We received "a Saviour, which is Christ the Lord" (Luke 2:11), a Savior who "is full of grace and truth" (2 Nephi 2:6), a Savior who chose to become like us so we can choose to become like Him.

Chapter 2

A COVENANT RELATIONSHIP

We have a secret code in our family—three hand squeezes means "I love you." When my son Russell was little, he always gave my hand five squeezes. I assumed he just couldn't count very well yet. Then one day I asked him what five squeezes meant, and he said, "I love you way much!"

Whenever I tell my little granddaughters I love them, they usually respond by saying, "We love you more!"

Then I say, "I love you the most."

Then, trying to top me, they say, "We love you from the heavens to the mud!" My little grandsons are not really speaking too much yet, so when I tell them I love them they usually just grunt and run off to find Grandma.

Young children understand love, and they know that for it to truly exist it takes at least two people. Grace is not one-sided

A COVENANT RELATIONSHIP

either. Like love, grace recognizes—even requires—a relationship. Elder Bruce C. Hafen and Marie K. Hafen wrote that many Christians see "grace as a one-way infusion, not as the two-way interaction it really is."[1]

Some Christians say grace is a gift that comes without any obligation. "Otherwise it is not a gift," they reason. However, in his book *Relational Grace*, Brent J. Schmidt, a religious education faculty member at BYU–Idaho, explained that grace is a gift that requires a response from us. He performed an in-depth analysis of the literary and cultural contexts out of which the Greek word *charis* emerged—the very word that was translated as *grace* or *favor* in our current scriptures. His conclusion was that anciently, grace was seen as a bond or pact between two people—even a binding covenant. It was a gift, but one that brought with it reciprocal obligations. He wrote, "Reciprocity is a gift-giving convention that is used almost universally by humanity to create social relationships."[2]

I am not an expert in ancient cultures or in the Greek language, but, like a child who understands love, it is easy for me to see that grace requires a relationship. It seems incomplete to receive a gift and not be able to respond in a way that the giver would appreciate.

> *Like love, grace recognizes—even requires—a relationship.*

That said, there are many reciprocal relationships that don't accurately reflect the relationship we have with God or the reasons for His expectations of us. I don't see God as a self-interested business partner or a covenant as a take-it-or-leave-it contract. I see a loving relationship.

After speaking of Alma's invitation for people to come into the fold of God and to be called His people, President Henry B. Eyring said, "Alma knew the covenant was not like a business deal—'you do this for God, and God will do this for you'—but it was an opportunity for them to become His, to become God's people. Every covenant with God is an opportunity to draw closer to Him."[3]

Similarly, author Truman G. Madsen has written, "Covenant keeping is not a cold business deal but a warm relationship."[4]

Perhaps the reciprocal relationship within which we receive the "grace he showeth" (*Hymns*, no. 299) is best understood using some of the descriptions provided by Jesus. He taught that His special relationship with us is similar to a nurturing adult and a child, a vine and a branch, companions yoked together, the good Samaritan and the injured traveler, and a bridegroom and a bride.

NURTURING ADULT AND CHILD

When Jesus said, "Suffer little children to come unto me" (Luke 18:16), He may not have had only children in mind.

A COVENANT RELATIONSHIP

When He gathered His Apostles together for the last time in His mortal life, He called them "little children" (John 13:33). These were grown men who were destined to change the world, yet Christ called them His little children. Relational grace can be seen in the context of a loving parent or caring teacher and a child.

I have been blessed with many wonderful teachers at every phase of my life, but Julia Golding was there for me at an important turning point. She was called to be my Primary teacher when I was eleven. She told the bishop she did not consider herself to be a very good teacher—especially for a class of all boys. Nevertheless, she accepted the call and served diligently. She often began her lessons by apologizing that we got "stuck" with her. Then she proceeded to touch the life of every boy with her love and testimony.

I remember her helping us memorize the Articles of Faith and various scriptures. I recall her enthusiastic retelling of stories from the scriptures and Church history. I can't hear the story of the conversion of Alma the Younger and the sons of Mosiah without thinking of how I felt as Sister Golding told it. I can't hear "A Poor Wayfaring Man of Grief" (*Hymns*, no. 29) without remembering the touching way she described Joseph Smith asking John Taylor to sing it in Carthage Jail. I remember her telling us how Heber J. Grant persevered to improve his handwriting and challenged us to always strive toward worthy goals.

Most of all, I remember how she reached out to me personally. I was not inactive, but she could see that I was not part of the circle of friendship the other boys enjoyed. I spent several childhood years in Ethiopia, Africa, where my father was working to improve the quality of education. Sports were not part of my life in Addis Ababa. When our family returned to the United States, I became painfully aware that I did not know how to play basketball, baseball, and football the way the other boys did. I felt excluded at school and church. Sister Golding reached out to include me.

I remember her showing interest in my interests. At the time, I was taking piano lessons and also spent hours drawing house plans. She asked me to play the songs I was learning for her and invited me to give her ideas as she remodeled her home. She "hired" me and another boy in the class, Lindsay, to help her sell apples at a roadside stand. Not only did that make me feel important, but it also gave me a lot of time to talk and bond with Lindsay, who became a good (and much needed) friend. I remember her making special arrangements for me to help with the Cub Scouts in the ward during their weekly meetings. Helping those younger children awakened in me a love of teaching that has lasted throughout my life.

Long after I left her class and she was released from her calling, Sister Golding continued to follow my progress. Not only would she greet me at church, but she would also call and praise me when I gave a talk or performed a musical number. When she heard of an accomplishment at school, she was quick to write me a little note. Even after our ward got divided and we did not attend meetings together, she came when I spoke in sacrament meeting as I left on my mission and when I returned. I continue to receive validating words and hugs whenever I see this remarkable woman, who recently turned one hundred. She reached out with love and acceptance when I was eleven, and I still feel her support today. She made a difference at a lonely and discouraging time in my life, and I will forever count myself blessed that I got "stuck" with her.

My relationship with Julia Golding helps me understand my covenant relationship with God. Was it a reciprocal relationship? Yes, but not in a win-win business arrangement sort of way. Julia certainly did not give so much to me because of what I offered in return. She got a piano recital that must have been painful for her to listen to and ideas for remodeling her home that were pretty outrageous (I think I suggested an indoor pool with her bed on an island in the middle of it). She also got help selling apples on the roadside, but none of that was a fair trade. Everything she asked of me was really just another way of helping me.

Everything she asked of me was really just another way of helping me.

Similarly, God does not give grace for what He can gain from us. As we live His commandments and strive to follow the example of Jesus, we are not giving Him a gift of equal or greater value. His expectations within our covenant relationship are primarily for our sakes. I can bring God joy and glory as I accept His nurturing hand in my life, just as I'm sure some of my antics made Julia Golding smile. I hope she is proud to tell people she was my teacher. Nevertheless, for both God and Julia, their joy and glory are consequences of the grace they offer—not their motivation.

VINE AND BRANCH

Jesus told His followers, "I am the vine, ye are the branches: He that abideth in me, and I in him, the same bringeth forth much fruit: for without me ye can do nothing" (John 15:5). When we think of reciprocal grace, we must consider the relationship between a vine and a branch. The vine provides nourishment. The expectation is growth and fruit—both of which would be impossible for the branch to produce without its vital connection to the vine.

Shortly after my first mission was over when I was a young man, a friend asked me to write a song that could be performed in the sacrament meeting where he was to speak before leaving on his own mission. I had just returned from serving in Chile Viña del Mar, which translates to "Vineyard of the Sea," so

A COVENANT RELATIONSHIP

Christ's teachings of vines, branches, and fruit were in the forefront of my mind when I wrote the following lyrics that Steven Kapp Perry put to music. I called the song "The True Vine":

> *I am the branch. Thou art the vine.*
> *I know I'll have strength as my hand is in Thine.*
> *Please nourish and help me to grow as I should*
> *And in turn I will promise Thee fruit that is good.*

Brent Fillmore teaches at the Institute of Religion adjacent to Utah State University. When he speaks to his classes of a covenant relationship, he talks about a stalactite hanging from the top of a cave dripping water on the floor below. In the water are minerals that soon start building up until they create a stalagmite reaching up toward the stalactite above. In time the two join and create a column or pillar. If we were to personify the relationship, the stalactite, like the vine, gives, and the stalagmite, like the branch, receives. The receiver reaches up as the giver reaches down.

The stalagmite is not self-sufficient. Without the stalactite, no growth is possible. Brother Fillmore says, "The very droplets from above contain within them the elements and minerals of the stalactite through which they have passed. Those minerals land on the stalagmite—drop by drop, line upon line—and help it grow like what is above it until they become one." He asks his students to stop running around and just be still like a stalagmite. "Just let yourselves get dripped on from above!" he tells them.

The nurturing relationship between a vine and branch or a stalactite and stalagmite helps me understand my covenant relationship with God. My job is not to do my part in order to receive grace, for there is nothing I can do in and of myself. In our relationship with the Lord, He declares, "My grace, all sufficient, shall be thy supply" (*Hymns*, no. 85). Paul taught that we must "work out [our] own salvation with fear and trembling," and then He added, "For it is God which worketh in you" (Philippians 2:12–13). In this reciprocal relationship, His expectation is that I accept the grace He offers—that I welcome it, grow, and pass it on.

COMPANIONS YOKED TOGETHER

Christ told His followers, "Come unto me, all ye that labour and are heavy laden, and I will give you rest. Take my yoke upon you, and learn of me; for I am meek and lowly in heart: and ye shall find rest unto your souls. For my yoke is easy, and my burden is light" (Matthew 11:28–30).

A yoke is a wooden crosspiece that is fastened over the necks of two animals and attached to a plow or cart they are to pull. Pioneers often yoked oxen together to pull their wagons. As we think of the Greek word *charis* and the reciprocal relationship it assumes, let us not think of one ox pulling and then

A COVENANT RELATIONSHIP

the other in turn. Let us think of two oxen pulling together. One may be much weaker than the other, but the yoke allows for a joining of forces, maximizing the strength of the two animals as they pull in unison.

Elder David A. Bednar taught, "Making and keeping sacred covenants yokes us to and with the Lord Jesus Christ."⁵ Together with Him, the burden becomes light because His strength is perfect (see 2 Corinthians 12:9). When He asks us to serve Him with "heart, might, mind and strength" (D&C 4:2), He is offering His heart, might, mind, and strength simultaneously.

When He asks us to serve Him with "heart, might, mind and strength" (D&C 4:2), He is offering His heart, might, mind, and strength simultaneously.

In addition to representing shared strength, in ancient Israel the image of the yoke also communicated discipleship. "Learn of me," the Savior said, "for I am meek" (Matthew 11:29). Meekness is the principle I was attempting to teach once at a youth conference after the young people had participated in doing baptisms for the dead in the temple. I pointed out that the baptismal font rests on the backs of twelve oxen—symbolic of the twelve tribes of Israel. One young woman raised her hand and asked, "Brother Wilcox, what is an ox?"

I glanced at some of the leaders in the group, wondering whether this was the time and place to go into all that, but with

35

their smiles of approval I launched into the explanation: "It's a bull that has been mellowed out," I stated. She (and most of the other youth) looked at me with blank faces. I tried again, "It is a bull that has been castrated" (Gulp! Did I just say that in a chapel?). In America we usually call a young, castrated bull a steer, but internationally it is called a bullock or an ox. "The ox is a perfect work animal," I explained, "because he has the strength of a bull, but he is no longer wild or dangerous." Meekness is not surrendering strength but surrendering stubborn willfulness.

The relationship between two animals yoked together helps me understand my covenant relationship with God as we work side by side. Not only because the yoke allows His strength to become mine, but because it symbolizes how He, in His meekness, is willing to teach me meekness as I serve at His side. My obligation in this reciprocal relationship is not to pull my share of the weight but rather to be meek and teachable as I receive His grace.

THE GOOD SAMARITAN AND THE INJURED TRAVELER

BYU professor John W. Welch has taught that the story of the good Samaritan can be seen as an allegory of the fall and redemption of mankind: a certain man (Adam) fell among thieves and was left for dead. Finally, a Samaritan—He who was hated of men (Christ)—saved him[6] (see Luke 10:25–35).

Then the Samaritan took the victim to an inn and paid for his care. The Samaritan had only one expectation of the injured traveler—that he would get well. Did the injured man thank him? Perhaps, but what if he had been unconscious? I can't imagine the Samaritan saying, "Why help him? He won't even know it was me."

After I shared this parable one year at BYU Campus Education Week, a young man said, "But the Samaritan had compassion on the injured man because he didn't get himself into the mess. He got robbed and beaten up. It wasn't his fault. I don't think Christ can have the same compassion on me when my messes are of my own making."

Would the good Samaritan have refused to help the man if he had slipped and fallen on his own? What if he had jumped off a cliff? I can't imagine the Samaritan saying, "Serves you right, then!" Would the Samaritan have withheld his assistance if the man had been overcome by heat instead of by thieves? I can't picture him saying, "It's your own fault for not wearing a hat and staying hydrated!" Doctors and nurses in hospitals have taken an oath to care for their patients even when they are prisoners, drunk drivers, or gang members.

Needs are needs no matter their origins (see Mosiah 4:17–18). If the Atonement were only for those who don't know better, then ignorance would be enviable rather than pitiable. Knowing the gospel would be a disadvantage rather than an advantage, and such is never the case. The uninformed will learn the gospel in the spirit world, and the innocent who die before the age of eight will one day have to grow until they are as knowledgeable and accountable as we are. Christ came to help all of us wherever we are in the process and for whatever reasons we need His help.

> Christ came to help all of us wherever we are in the process and for whatever reasons.

If knowing better condemns us when it comes to being "diligent in keeping his commandments," then let us also acknowledge that it saves us when it comes "to a knowledge of the goodness of God, and his matchless power, and his wisdom, and his patience, and his long-suffering towards the children of men; and also, the atonement which has been prepared from the foundation of the world" (Mosiah 4:6). Knowledge is always desirable (see D&C 130:19).

The relationship between the good Samaritan and the injured traveler helps me understand my covenant relationship with God. It is reciprocal, but that does not mean we are both on equal ground in our ability to contribute. The Samaritan gave grace because he could. The injured man received because he was in need. He simply could not save himself. Such an arrangement does not always describe good business, but it does describe goodness.

A COVENANT RELATIONSHIP

BRIDEGROOM AND BRIDE

Christ sometimes referred to His relationship with us as a marriage (see John 3:29). Married couples become one in purpose just as Christ desires to become one with us. As we partake of the sacrament, we covenant to take the Lord's name upon us as a bride takes the name of a bridegroom.

One young bride-to-be was concerned about taking her husband's last name as their wedding got closer. She felt that she was giving up part of herself and complained that it wasn't fair. Why didn't her fiancé take her last name instead? She found many opinions posted on the Internet that claimed the traditional practice is outdated and even demeaning to women. The girl asked friends and family members what they thought, and someone said, "It's a sign you love your husband."

She asked, "Well, why doesn't he take my name as a sign he loves me?"

Someone else added, "It shows you belong to him."

She exploded, "What? Like I'm his slave or something?" The closer she came to her marriage, the more she resisted the idea of changing her name.

Finally, she and her fiancé spoke with their bishop about the dilemma. He listened and then explained, "Many traditions we associate with marriage mean little in today's culture because they have lost their original religious significance. For example, what color is your wedding dress?"

"White, of course," the young woman answered.

"Why?" the bishop asked. The girl and her fiancé had never even thought about it. The bishop said, "Brides wear white to symbolize purity—just like we wear white when we are baptized and go to the temple. It's too bad so few people in today's world think—or live—that way. They just wear white because of tradition."

The bishop continued, "It's the same with a wife taking her husband's name. The act actually symbolizes the covenant relationship Christ has with us as members of His Church. The bridgegroom represents Christ, and the bride represents the Church. In Ephesians 5:25 we read, 'Husbands, love your wives, even as Christ also loved the church, and gave himself for it.'" The bishop said, "The taking and giving of Christ's name is reminiscent of the covenants made in baptism and in the temple through which Christ can 'sanctify and cleanse [us] . . . that [we] should be holy and without blemish.' It symbolizes how He 'nourisheth and cherisheth' us (Ephesians 5:26–27, 29). When Paul taught, 'For this cause shall a man leave his father and mother, and shall be joined unto his wife, and they two shall be one flesh,' he wasn't just speaking about marriage. Paul himself said, 'I speak concerning Christ and the church'" (Ephesians 5:31–32).

That was the perspective this young couple had been missing. With this new understanding in their hearts, the young woman gladly took her husband's name, not because the couple was jumping through some meaningless, traditional hoop, but because the act symbolized the covenant relationship they both had with Christ.

The relationship between a bridegroom and his bride helps me understand my covenant relationship with God. Marriage is not a contract between Party A and Party B. It is an institution in which the whole is greater than the sum of the parts. As we willingly take Christ's name, He willingly gives it, together with His grace. Our obligation is to stay faithful and to never leave Him, just as He promises to never leave us. Our motivation is the deep love we feel for each other. Together with Him, we can become more than we can be on our own.

President Ezra Taft Benson declared, "Men and women who turn their lives over to God will discover that He can make a lot more out of their lives than they can. He will deepen their joys, expand their vision, quicken their minds, strengthen their muscles, lift their spirits, multiply their blessings, increase their opportunities, comfort their souls, raise up friends, and pour out peace."[7]

Whether we think of Christ as a nurturing adult, vine, companion, good Samaritan, or bridegroom, we are always dependent on Him and better because of Him. Of course, I have been selective in the examples I have chosen to share in this chapter. There are many other metaphors and parables in the scriptures that actually move in opposite directions. At times

Jesus also cast Himself as a steward (see Luke 12:42), employer (see Matthew 20:1), judge (see Luke 12:58), and landlord (see Mark 12:9). I've presented business partners as negative and contractual agreements as straitjackets. Obviously, many business contacts and contracts are friendly and mutually beneficial. I have presented family and teacher-student relationships as positive, although some are full of antagonism, manipulation, and spite. All relationships can be complex, and relational grace is no exception. The main point is that grace is a two-way interaction. The question isn't whether or not God's grace requires something of us, but why, and to what end? The reciprocal nature of grace means we are obligated, but not to fulfill our end of a bargain as much as to build and strengthen a relationship.

One Christian friend told me, "If grace takes work, it is not grace." I guess if I saw grace as a one-sided gift—a plate of cookies dropped anonymously on my doorstep—I might feel the same. However, Brent J. Schmidt's research of the Greek word for grace (*charis*) and the Hebrew word for grace (*hesed*) showed that they only existed within covenant relationships. For many Christians, God has become so immaterial that they struggle to understand what it means to have a relationship with such a distant and

> *Grace is a two-way interaction.*

A COVENANT RELATIONSHIP

remote being. It has become easy for them to separate the gift from the giver to such a point that they take them both for granted. Latter-day Saints know the nature of God at such an intimate and personal level that we feel a bond with Him that quickly overshadows any sense of deservedness or entitlement. Covenants are seen as "an exchange of love between us and our Heavenly Father."[8]

All relationships require something of those involved, but when those relationships are healthy, the obligations are met in the context of love. It is love that allows us to see beyond the requirements to the joy, purpose, and meaning provided by the relationship. It is the same with God. Those who choose to maintain a covenant relationship with Him by coming into His fold, remembering Him always, and striving to keep His commandments choose to be changed through His grace. The requirement to lose themselves in His service is superseded by the opportunity to find themselves in His love (see Matthew 10:39).

Chapter 3

RECEIVING GRACE

Robert Robinson was a small boy in the 1730s when his father died and he had to work to help support the family. As a teenager, he fell in with a bad group of friends and lived a wild and worldly lifestyle. One day Robert and his buddies heard that a renowned minister was scheduled to preach in a nearby church, and they decided to attend and heckle him. When the preacher began, however, Robert was captivated by his sermon, and instead of heckling, he left the meeting determined to repent.

At the age of twenty, Robert set out to become a minister himself. Two years later, in 1757, he wrote a hymn expressing gratitude for the divine grace that helped him change his misguided life: "Come thou fount of every blessing, tune my heart to sing thy grace; Streams of mercy never ceasing call for songs of loudest praise" (lds.org/music/text).

My favorite line in the text is, "O to grace how great a debtor daily I'm constrained to be!" Robinson recognized he was in debt to God for His grace. King Benjamin taught his people the same principle and told them that even if they tried to repay God by keeping commandments, they would still be unprofitable servants. The minute they obeyed, God would bless them and they would be "indebted unto him, and are, and will be, forever and ever" (Mosiah 2:24).

Receiving grace is like receiving a scholarship. It doesn't guarantee learning. It facilitates it.

Both Robert Robinson and King Benjamin emphasized our indebtedness to God, but what we must understand clearly is that God couldn't care less about getting paid back. His joy is found in seeing us value His gift. Receiving grace is like receiving a scholarship. It doesn't guarantee learning. It facilitates it. The scholarship donor doesn't want the money back. He or she wants it utilized.

LEVELS OF GRACE

When my grandchildren are born, one of the first things I do for them is present them with their first books and read to them. I want them surrounded with books and language and love from day one! As the children have grown I have continued to read to them, and now some are old enough to read books to me—which I love. When they do, I hug them and promptly give them more books!

These interactions help me understand how God gives us His grace: "I will give unto the children of men line upon line, precept upon precept . . . ; and blessed are those who hearken unto my precepts, and lend an ear unto my counsel, for they shall learn wisdom; for unto him that receiveth I will give more" (2 Nephi 28:30).

The parable of the talents can have many interpretations, including the development of gifts and talents and preparing for the Second Coming. My daughter Whitney explained to me how it can also be viewed as a parable about receiving grace.[1] Now when I read Matthew 25, I no longer think just of money or abilities. I think of books: And unto one he gave five books, to another two books, and to another one book. The first two read their books and the lord said, "Well done. You have read a few books. I will now give you more. Enter into my library!" The third servant didn't care about his book so the lord ended up taking it away—not because he was being mean or punishing the servant. He took the book away because the servant had already tossed it aside. What good is a book to one who refuses to read? Many missionaries have felt the pain of giving away a copy of the Book of Mormon only to see it discarded by the recipient. This choice says more about the person making it than it does about the missionaries or the book. In the parable, even if the lord had welcomed the third servant into his library, the servant would not have valued anything there. Until he changed his attitude, additional books would have been more burden than blessing.

So it is with receiving grace. "For unto him that receiveth it shall be given more abundantly, even power" (D&C 71:6). But "from them that shall say, We have enough, from them shall be taken away even that which they have" (2 Nephi 28:30).

I used to be confused by the many descriptions of God's power found throughout the scriptures. They speak of grace as enabling power (see Matthew 8:17) but also the light of Christ as power (see D&C 88:13). We read of the power of faith (see Alma 18:35), the power of the Holy Ghost (see Moroni 10:7), and power from on high promised in temples (see D&C 38:32; 105:11). Scriptures also teach of the power of the priesthood (see D&C 113:8), "the greatest power on earth."[2] I couldn't figure out where one ended and the others began.

Finally, I realized that "there is no other power, save the power of God" (D&C 8:7; see also Romans 13:1). Different labels for God's power do not describe different powers, but varying amounts, uses, and aspects of the same power. For example, a young child who is baptized receives the gift of the Holy Ghost. Years later that same child enters the temple and receives a greater endowment of the Spirit that brings with it greater rights and responsibilities.

Even the Savior "received not of the fulness at first, but continued from grace to grace, until he received a fulness" (D&C 93:13). Richard D. Draper, BYU professor of ancient scripture, wrote, "The Lord . . . went from one power level to another, from one capacity to a greater, until he received a fullness of the Father."[3] It appears God gives His children power similarly to how I give my grandchildren books. Those who use what they receive are granted more. The Savior said, "I give unto you . . . that you may come unto the Father in my name, and in due time receive of his fulness" (D&C 93:19). No wonder we sing, "Our God is pleased when we improve his grace" (*Hymns*, no. 240) and "the knowledge and power of God are expanding" (*Hymns*, no. 2).

GRACE TO GRACE

When converts first join the Church, we do not tell them to leave behind everything they have previously learned about God and grace. On the contrary, our message is, "Bring with you all the good that you have, and then let us see if we can add to it."[4]

As new members continue to exercise faith and repent, they receive more grace (see Mosiah 18:10). Each time they partake of the sacrament, they engage with God in utilizing His gifts and welcome more grace into their lives. Soon they enter temples, where they make additional covenants showing they are willing and ready to receive even more grace.

By participating in priesthood ordinances, we exercise our agency and elect to receive additional divine power. In the hymn "God of Power, God of Right," we sing, "Lift us step by step to thee thru an endless ministry" (*Hymns*, no. 20). Joseph Smith taught, "You have got to learn how to be Gods yourselves . . . by going from one small degree to another, and from a small capacity to a great one; from grace to grace, from exaltation to exaltation."[5]

Latter-day Saints do not perform priesthood ordinances as empty works in place of faith but as inevitable outgrowths of it. They are more than symbolic rituals. "They constitute authorized channels through which the blessings and powers of heaven can flow into our individual lives. . . . Ordinances received and honored with integrity are essential to obtaining the power of godliness and all of the blessings made available through the Savior's Atonement."[6] Making covenants is not a declaration that we don't need grace but an indication that we are ready to receive more.

Making covenants is not a declaration that we don't need grace but an indication that we are ready to receive more.

Some Christians say ordinances are unnecessary works because we are saved by grace, but ordinances are not acts of earning, qualifying, or meriting grace. They are acts of accepting and receiving it. Those who listen carefully during the endowment hear the word *receive* many times. In the endowment we do not see portrayals of Christ in Gethsemane, on the cross, or leaving the tomb, because the endowment is not about how Christ *gave* us the Atonement. Rather, "the story of Adam and Eve is the story of *receiving* and engaging His Atonement."[7] We receive grace the same way Adam and Eve did—under the direction of those who possess priesthood keys (see D&C 13:1; 29:42) and by choosing to make and keep covenants.

In the Doctrine and Covenants we read the phrase *new and everlasting covenant* (see 22:1; 131:2; 132:4), which does not refer only to baptism or temple marriage, as some have taught. Rather, it refers to the sum total of *all* covenants and obligations found within the fullness of the gospel.[8] *Everlasting* means these covenants are unchanging and span eternity (see D&C 132:7). *New* means they have been restored in our day.

Elder Marcus B. Nash has taught, "To the degree we thoughtfully and faithfully keep the covenants associated with the ordinances we receive, we will grow in our knowledge of God and experience the 'power of godliness' (D&C 84:20–21) by the grace of God through the Atonement of Christ."[9] As we make sacred covenants to keep "the law of obedience and sacrifice, the law of the gospel, the law of chastity, and the law of consecration,"[10] we can participate in sealings. With each covenant, we receive more and more of the divine help from God we call grace.

OBEDIENCE AND SACRIFICE

We show we value Christ's obedience and sacrifice as we are willing to engage with Him in obeying and sacrificing in like manner. When Debi and I served our mission in Chile, we witnessed many sweet and selfless sacrifices. In the April 2004 general conference, Elder Jeffrey R. Holland said, "I wish you could meet the sister called to serve [in Chile] from her native Argentina. Wanting to do everything possible to finance her own mission, she sold her violin, her most prized and nearly sole earthly possession. She said simply, 'God will bless me with another violin after I have blessed His children with the gospel of Jesus Christ.'"[11]

Listeners across the world did not know this sister missionary was serving in our mission at the time, but we did. Imagine the sister's surprise when by the next zone conference the missionaries throughout the mission had pooled their limited resources and purchased a violin for her. She was overwhelmed when they presented her with the gift.

Another time I received a phone call from a man I'd never met who said, "President, do any of your missionaries need new clothing?" I explained that although there were elders and sisters with needs, it was expensive to ship large packages and they rarely made it through customs. He said, "I'm not planning on sending a package. I'm going to bring it with me." He was a pilot, and whenever he got his flight schedule he would call the mission president where he was going and ask for a list of needs. Members of his high priest group would then help him fill the requests, and he would deliver the clothing when he flew in. Sure enough, within the week there were elders in the mission with new shirts, sisters with new blouses, and one elder with a new pair of size fifteen shoes that were impossible for him to get in Chile.

On another occasion, the mother of one of the missionaries wrote and explained a service project she and her friends wanted to do. She had heard that the Santiago Chile Temple was being remodeled and the Saints had been encouraged to purchase their own temple clothes for when it reopened. She said, "President, I know that even with the Church subsidizing most of the cost, there will be some faithful members who will not be able to afford the clothing. We want to help." And help they did! By December 25, every missionary in our mission received a complete set of temple clothes he or she could in turn present to a worthy but needy member. The missionaries dubbed the project "White Christmas."

These are just a few of the sacrifices that touched our hearts while we served. No doubt many missionaries and mission presidents treasure similar memories. Long ago, the faithful sacrificed animals. Today they quietly place violins, size fifteen shoes, and white temple clothes on the altar. The "what" of sacrifice has changed, but the "why" remains the same. It is done in similitude of the sacrifice of the Savior (see Moses 5:7) and to invite into our lives the very grace that can make us similar to Him.

When Christ came to ancient America He told the people they were no longer to offer animals, but

The "what" of sacrifice has changed, but the "why" remains the same.

"a broken heart and a contrite spirit" (3 Nephi 9:20). Centuries later, people fell into apostasy and this teaching was twisted to the point that priests performed human sacrifices and offered the broken hearts—literally—of their victims to God. We would never dream of making such horrific sacrifices today, but until we have been changed through grace we sometimes offer our sacrifices with the same motives as the apostate priests. Do we feel we must sacrifice to appease an angry God and keep His punishments at bay, or do we sacrifice out of love? Are we paying tithing as "fire insurance" so we don't burn at the Second Coming or because of the fire of testimony burning within us? Do we obey commandments in an effort to earn the Savior's blessings or to emulate His life?

I know a woman who no longer considers herself LDS. She

said, "I went to seminary, read my scriptures, kept the Word of Wisdom, and did everything else that good little Mormon girls are supposed to do. When it was time for me to get married, no returned missionary showed up to whisk me off to the temple. I did everything right and where did it get me?"

I felt sorry for her loneliness, but I also was concerned about her motivation. Were her sacrifices just about getting a husband? Did she assume she was putting money in some big bank account in the sky so she could make a withdrawal when it was time to get married? When God didn't "pay up," was she justified in "showing Him" by refusing to sacrifice anymore?

I share this woman's story because it is actually all of our stories—not the details, but the theme. We have all been disappointed when our sacrifices did not bring forth the blessings of heaven—at least not the ones we desired (see *Hymns*, no. 27). Because our expectations were not met, we felt overlooked, mistreated, and tempted to pull away from God.

In such moments we must instead draw closer to God through continued obedience and sacrifice. As we do, grace helps us learn humility, purify our motives, and expand our expectations. My friend Brent Fillmore encourages his institute students to change their thinking by changing their words. I've tried to follow his advice. Instead of saying, "*If* I obey, God will bless me," I've begun to say, "As I obey, He will bless me." Instead of saying, "*When* I sacrifice, He will bless me," I've begun to say, "*While* I sacrifice, He will bless me." This is one simple way we can invite God to broaden our vision to include His will as well as ours, to focus on a process as well as a product, and to consider the journey as well as the destination. As we covenant to obey and sacrifice, we invite more of God's power into our lives.

GOSPEL

Along with living the law of obedience and sacrifice, we are also expected to live the gospel. We show we value the gospel Jesus Christ taught as we are willing to engage with Him in living it.

The word *gospel* comes from the Old English word *godspell*—*god* meaning good and *spell* meaning story or news. The gospel means good news! Jesus Christ came and lived a perfect life, completed the Atonement, and lives again. These realities and blessings are good news indeed, but surely the good news also includes the Restoration, the first principles and ordinances, priesthood keys, temples, and—though few think of it like this—rules! Gospel laws and standards are part of the good news and some of our greatest evidences of God's love.

One single mother was struggling to rear her children in the gospel after her husband left the Church and divorced her. She told me tearfully how difficult it was to be the "bad guy" who enforced bedtimes, stressed nutrition, and required church attendance while her ex-husband did the opposite. On the weekends the children were with him, he let them stay up late and eat whatever they wanted, and he took them to amusement parks instead of church.

I assured her she was doing the right thing even though it was difficult. Just two weeks later this mother shared with me a note her oldest daughter had written: "Dear Mom, Thanks for being our mom. Dad is just trying to be our buddy. He is trying to win us over by spending money on us, but I am old enough to see what is going on and I appreciate you for expecting us to make something of our lives. Maybe the little kids don't get it yet, but I do. The parent with the rules is the one who really cares."

> *The parent with the rules is the one who really cares.*

Heavenly Father expects us to make something out of our lives. His rules show He really cares and doesn't want us to waste our time and opportunities to grow. To ask God to revise or suspend commandments would be asking Him to stop loving us, and He cannot do that. Instead, He sends His grace to help us see the bigger picture.

In Alma 12:32 we read, "Therefore God gave unto them commandments, after having made known unto them the plan of redemption." The restoration of the gospel was not a restoration of rules. It was a restoration of reasons. The Ten Commandments and the Sermon on the Mount actually made it through the Apostasy; it was the reasons to keep the commandments and live the lessons taught in the sermon that were lost. Those reasons, as Alma explained, are found within the plan of redemption. They have to do with changing internal desires as well as external behavior, altering the way we live in private as well as in public. Such changes come only through God's grace. As we covenant to live the gospel, we invite a greater abundance of God's power into our lives.

CHASTITY

In addition to obeying, sacrificing, and living the gospel, God asks us to live the law of chastity. We show we value God and Christ's purity as we are willing to engage with them in living chaste lives.

Satan and his followers will never have bodies. No wonder they tempt us to misuse ours. They will never have marriages or families. No wonder they attack those of us who do. Breaking the law of chastity weakens and destroys marriages and families and allows Satan to take one more giant step toward making us miserable like he is (see 2 Nephi 2:27).

The world would convince us that by choosing to remain chaste we are missing something—that the Church is holding us back. But God is not asking us to be chaste because He doesn't want us to be happy or feel satisfied. He asks us to keep sexual desires and expressions within the bounds He sets because He knows that it is only within those bounds that true joy and satisfaction are found. He is not keeping us from something. He is offering us everything! Research shows that those who live together before marriage have higher divorce rates and lower satisfaction in marriage than those who don't. Similarly, the more sexual partners people have before marriage, the lower their satisfaction in marriage.[12]

People who choose to live out of bounds often brag about how they are getting something great, but the facts don't support their claims. If what they get is so great, then why are they rarely satisfied? Why do so many go from Internet site to Internet site, bed to bed, partner to partner, and gender to gender? If what they have is as wonderful as they make it out to be, why are they continually searching? Why are they not content? Their boasts may be simply an attempt to convince themselves they are happier than they really are. Look at happily married couples. They aren't usually looking (or bragging) because they have the true love, oneness, and satisfaction everyone else seeks so desperately.

A fire kept within bounds can be used to warm and feed you. It can light your way. A fire out of bounds can burn down the whole house and everyone in it. This is why Alma told his son, "See that ye bridle all your passions." He did not say passions are evil or bad—only that they must be bridled. A powerful horse does not reach its potential by being allowed to run wild. Sex can only be as good as it can possibly be within the bonds of marriage between a man and a woman where love, trust, and fidelity abound. "Bridle all your passions," Alma said, "that ye may be filled with love" (Alma 38:12). Love! The very emotion that so many use to justify immoral choices can be the force that keeps us from making them—love for ourselves, our spouses, our children, and for our Lord.

Living this way requires more strength than we can muster on our own. It requires grace. By setting bounds, God is not controlling us but teaching and empowering us to control ourselves. He is changing us so we can live as He lives and feel the joy He feels. As we covenant to be chaste, we invite more of God's power into our lives.

CONSECRATION

Obeying, sacrificing, living the gospel, and honoring the law of chastity are all preparation for (and symbols of) living the law of consecration. We show we value all God gives to us as we engage with Him and give our time, talents, and treasure to His kingdom.

I recall when Sister Janice Kapp Perry, who has written so many beloved songs for the Church, said, "Brad, are you at that point yet?"

I responded, "What point?"

She said, "The point when being invited to speak, teach, write, and travel is not always as fun as it once was." I assured her

I was long past that point. She smiled and said, "Good! That's when you know you are living a consecrated life." Sister Perry has learned by her own experience that there is a difference between giving God your things and giving Him yourself. It is one thing to lay an animal on the altar and another to lay ourselves there. Sacrifice is putting ourselves in the place of Abraham. Consecration is putting ourselves in the place of Isaac.

Three years after Sister Elaine S. Dalton was released as Young Women general president, I was privileged to speak at the same Time Out for Women event where she was presenting. Her talk and testimony were beautiful, but more important to me was watching the sincere and genuine way she greeted young women before and after the event. I knew she was exhausted, but that didn't stop her from listening, lifting, and loving others.

On our way to the airport, someone said to her, "Sister Dalton, why do you wear yourself out like this when it is no longer your calling?"

She said, "But it *is* my calling. I am a disciple of Jesus Christ with temple covenants to keep." Sister Dalton did not begin caring about young women when she was called to be their president. She did not stop because she was released. She may no longer sit on the stand in general conference, but she continues to stand as a witness of God wherever she goes. Her example inspires me.

Christ said those who receive His servants receive Him, and those who receive Him receive His Father, and those who receive the Father receive all that the Father has (see D&C 84:36–38). It sounds like everything is leading up to some big payday in the sky—until we connect the word *receive* with words like *value* and *appreciate*. Those who *value* prophets value Christ, and those who *appreciate* Christ appreciate His Father and all His Father has.

Imagine that a wealthy man passes away and his greedy family members gather to get their hands on his fortune. One granddaughter doesn't care about that. She asks for only a painting that hung in her grandfather's study. She knew he loved it, and it reminds her of him. The family is happy to sign an agreement giving her the painting because that means more money for them! The day finally comes that the lawyer reveals the contents of the wealthy man's bank account, and the family is shocked to discover it is almost empty. Turns out, years earlier the old man had invested most of his money in the purchase of a rare painting—the very one the family had just signed over to the only family member who wanted it. Because the granddaughter loved what her grandfather had loved, she received all he had. As we covenant to consecrate ourselves, we learn to love what God loves and invite more of His power into our lives.

SEALINGS

All other covenants and ordinances prepare us for the crowning ordinance of the temple: sealings. As we are sealed as families in the temple, we willingly engage with Him in creating eternal families—not just on paper, but in actuality.

None of us is born already destined to become like Satan or Christ. We are all born innocent and free to choose to become like either. Those who choose to follow Satan soon find that "the devil hath all power over [them]" (Alma 34:35), whereas those who choose to follow Christ discover He shares all power with them (see D&C 132:19).

None of us is born already destined to become like Satan or Christ. We are all born innocent and free to choose to become like either.

Satan and Christ both want us to be sealed to them eternally. Alma warned, "For behold, if ye have procrastinated the day of your repentance . . . ye have become subjected to the spirit of the devil, and he doth seal you his" (Alma 34:35). However, King Benjamin taught, "Therefore, I would that ye should be steadfast and immovable, . . . that Christ, the Lord God Omnipotent, may seal you his" (Mosiah 5:15). Ultimately, we choose to whom we want to be sealed.

God will always be the Father of our spirits. As His begotten spirit children, we were born within His everlasting covenant in our premortal state. Those who rejected that covenant then rejected His grace and distanced themselves from God. Those who reject it in mortality and those who reject it in the spirit world are also choosing to separate themselves from God and no longer be sealed to Him. Those who accept His grace engage with Him in overcoming the world by faith and remain sealed to Him as part of His eternal family (see D&C 76:53). When we sing "Families Can Be Together Forever" (*Hymns*, no. 300), we usually think only of husbands and wives, children and parents, as they have lived on this earth. This sometimes causes people to worry about what will happen in cases of divorce or second or third marriages. People also worry about those who have never had the opportunity to marry and family members who do not stay worthy. We can find comfort in remembering that God, who knows all things, will sort out even the most complex of situations. We can find additional comfort when we remember that there is another eternal family to which we can also choose to be sealed, and that is the family of our Heavenly Parents (see D&C 76:24).

In ancient Israel, outsiders could become insiders through covenants. As they made covenants they became "kin."[13] By choosing to remain in a covenant relationship with God, we choose to remain sealed to Him.

Children here on earth can be born under the covenant, but we realize that status speaks only of possibilities. The realization of being an eternal family depends on the choices of those involved. Being born in the covenant does not guarantee we will be sealed to earthly parents. The same can be said of our relationship with God. When we have lived so as to see potential realized, then that sealing is confirmed by "the Holy Spirit of promise" (D&C 76:53) and becomes a reality. This will truly make us joint-heirs with Christ in every sense of the word. Scriptures describe this as the moment when we are adopted by God (see Galatians 4:5). Just as adopted children on earth can be sealed to their parents, this heavenly adoption allows us to remain sealed to Heavenly Parents. Paul taught, "Ye have received the Spirit of adoption, . . . and if children, then heirs; heirs of God, and joint-heirs with Christ" (Romans 8:15–17).

Author Robert L. Millet wrote, "In him is the power which may be extended . . . to become the sons and daughters of God, the means whereby we may [receive] . . . our status in the royal family of God."[14] Exaltation is not earned. It is inherited (see D&C 88:107). As we choose to stay sealed to God and have that sealing confirmed by the Holy Spirit of promise, then we will become members of what scriptures call the Church of the Firstborn, which allows us to inherit all that the Father has and become all that He and our Heavenly Mother are.[15] This would not be possible without grace. In fact, it is the ultimate purpose for and expression of God's grace.

This understanding gives new meaning to familiar scriptures: "But as many as received him, to them gave he power to become the sons [and daughters] of God" (John 1:12); "For God so loved the world, that he gave his only begotten Son, that whosoever believeth in him should not perish" (John 3:16); and Jesus "so loved the world that he gave his own life, that as many as would believe might become the sons [and daughters] of God" (D&C 34:3) and "that by him, and through him, and of him, the worlds are and were created, and the inhabitants thereof are begotten sons and daughters unto God" (D&C 76:24).

> *Too many in the world are settling for so little when they could have so much. Too many in the Church are settling for much when they could have a fullness.*

When Robert Robinson penned "Come Thou Fount of Every Blessing," he was inspired beyond his twenty-two-year-old understanding, for he wrote of sealings clear back in the 1700s: "Prone to wander Lord I feel it, prone to leave the God I love. Here's my heart, O *take and seal it, seal it* for thy courts above" (emphasis added). As we engage with God and Christ in receiving gospel ordinances and keeping the associated covenants, we progress from grace to grace and ultimately receive a "fulness" (D&C 109:15; see also Moroni 7:48). Too many in the world are settling for so little when they could have so much. Too many in the Church are settling for much when they could have a fullness. As sacred ordinances are sealed by the Holy Spirit of Promise (see D&C 76:52–53), we can be sealed to each other and to God forever.

Chapter 4

THE SPIRIT: MESSENGER OF GRACE

"I love the spirit of adventure in life," said Elder Robert E. Wells in general conference. When I heard the talk I had just recently graduated from Brigham Young University and was a young father. I was captivated as Elder Wells spoke of jaguars, alligators, and waterskiing on rivers full of man-eating piranha fish. Elder Wells told of flying his own airplane across continents and going on expeditions into danger-filled Amazon jungles. The movie *Raiders of the Lost Ark* had come out a few years earlier, and it seemed to me that Elder Wells was an LDS Indiana Jones! "I love the spirit of adventure," he declared. "But I love more the adventures of the Spirit."[1]

I also love the adventures of the Spirit. I've never piloted an airplane or run into jaguars in the Amazon, but I have had soul-stirring adventures with the Spirit that have changed me.

THE SPIRIT: MESSENGER OF GRACE

In Ether 12:41 we read that grace can come from "God the Father, and also the Lord Jesus Christ, *and the Holy Ghost*" (emphasis added). Elder Neal A. Maxwell taught that "applying the Atonement" is accepting the "nurturing gifts of the Holy Ghost."[2] One of the times I was especially grateful for those nurturing gifts happened in Rome, Italy. It was a moment when I saw how personally God is involved in our lives and recognized how His Spirit acts as the messenger of grace.

GOD'S HAND

My wife and I were scheduled to direct a tour group tracing the footsteps of the Apostle Paul throughout the Mediterranean. Several weeks before we left, my friend Ugo A. Perego, who works for Seminaries and Institutes in Italy, contacted me and asked if I would speak at a fireside when our group was scheduled to be in Rome. "We will translate your talk," he explained, "and broadcast it to youth and young single adults at various chapels throughout the country."

I agreed, and Brother Perego requested that I write down what I planned to say and send a copy in advance so the translator could prepare for the broadcast. I complied and looked forward to a great evening in Rome.

When the night finally came, Brother Perego picked me up at my hotel and drove me to the chapel. I greeted the young people and leaders who were gathering and met the sister who would be translating. She showed me well-marked and highlighted copies of my talk in English and Italian. I thanked her for her extra effort and took my place on the stand. The minute I sat down, the Spirit prompted me to change my talk. It is common for me to receive little promptings to alter what I have prepared based on the needs of those listening, but not to change my entire talk—especially at the last minute. I tried to ignore the prompting, but it was clear.

Somewhere in the middle of the opening hymn, I finally had the courage to lean toward Brother Perego and say, "I need to change my talk."

He tried to camouflage his surprise and whispered, "But the topic has been announced for weeks."

I cringed inside as I said, "I know, but I need to change my talk."

Brother Perego said, "But it has already been translated, and we are broadcasting live."

I said, "I know, but I need to change my talk. Is the translator good enough to wing it?"

I don't know what kind of bodily harm Brother Perego was planning to inflict on me after the meeting, but he calmly went to the side of the room and talked to the translator, who almost fainted. I thought, *Why are you doing this, Brad? What's the big deal? One talk or another, it's all the same gospel message. Why are you causing such a problem for everyone?* Yet, even as I questioned myself, I knew the answer. Some spiritual impressions are strong and consistent.

After I was introduced, I stood at the podium and said, "Tonight I would like to talk about why we believe in Christ." The translator did a masterful job keeping up with me, and we forged ahead. I spoke of how Latter-day Saints do not simply believe in Christ because of Christian heritage, the Bible, or history alone. We believe because of Joseph Smith, the Book of Mormon, living prophets and apostles, and because of the Spirit's assurance that we are not wrong.

Some spiritual impressions are strong and consistent.

After the fireside I enjoyed visiting with the young people and met several investigators who were in attendance. Then I noticed four young elders standing toward the back of the chapel and stepped closer to say hello. Before I could even ask where they were from, one elder blurted, "Why did you change your talk tonight?"

I thought, *Great! They were expecting the announced topic and now they are disappointed.* I said, "Sorry if I messed you up, but I just felt prompted to change it. Maybe it was for the sake of the investigators who attended."

The elder replied, "It wasn't for the investigators. You

changed your talk because we have been fasting all day that you would."

The elder then pointed to one of the other missionaries, who said, "Earlier this week I took a train to the mission office and told the mission president I wanted to go home. He asked his assistants to bring me here tonight hoping you would answer my question."

"And what was your question?" I asked.

He responded quietly, "I wondered why we even believe in Christ." I embraced him, and he started to cry. The other missionaries and I began to cry too. He continued, "I wondered why I am out here. I know it's for Christ, but then I started wondering why we even believe in Christ. I mean, can anyone prove He's real? I just didn't see the point in continuing with this charade when I don't even know if God is there or if He loves me."

I looked into the tear-filled eyes of this struggling elder and said, "Whenever you wonder if God is there and if He loves you, remember this moment. Remember God dragged me halfway around the world to hug you and that He prompted me to change my talk at the last minute for you. Now, go call your mission president and tell him you are staying!"

He and his companions did just that. His doubts and questions were many, but we worked through them as best we could via e-mails. That young man finished his mission strong.

THE SPIRIT: MESSENGER OF GRACE

In one of his final e-mails, he wrote, "I don't even want to think about what would have happened had I gone home when I wanted to. That night in Rome was evidence to me of God's existence and of His grace."

I wrote back, "I am glad you recognize that only God could have orchestrated that moment."

We both knew we had been involved in what Elder Robert E. Wells would have called an adventure of the Spirit, and we were both better for it. When most people think of Rome they think of the Colosseum or the Vatican. I think of an LDS chapel, a patient Brother Perego, a panicked translator, and four elders standing in the back fasting for a miracle. For many tourists, Rome means the Trevi Fountain. For me, Rome means a different fountain: "And my Spirit's grace shall be like a fountain unto thee" (*Hymns*, no. 185).

RECOGNIZING THE HOLY GHOST

The Holy Ghost is the third member of the Godhead and a personage of Spirit. He fills multiple roles for us. He is a witness of God and Christ and reveals truth. He is a comforter, guide, and sanctifier, to name only a few. We don't experience His roles in sequence. Our needs dictate when one role may be more prominent than the others. In all these roles the Spirit acts as the messenger of grace as He provides divine assistance and power.

In 2 Corinthians 9:14–15 Paul wrote of "the exceeding grace of God in you" and then wrote, "Thanks be unto God for his unspeakable gift." New Testament commentaries link the two verses together, saying that God's grace is too wonderful for words. However, the only other time the phrase *unspeakable gift* is mentioned in the standard works is in Doctrine and Covenants 121:26, where we read of "the unspeakable gift of the Holy Ghost." The two references demonstrate a clear connection between the Holy Ghost and grace. Elder D. Todd Christofferson taught that the "'power of godliness' comes in the person and by the influence of the Holy Ghost. . . . It is the messenger of grace by which the blood of Christ is applied."3

The Spirit acts as the messenger of grace as He provides divine assistance and power.

God loves all His children, and the influence of the Spirit can be felt by everyone, but it can pass into and out of people's lives like air passes into and out of a balloon. When we receive the gift of the Holy Ghost after baptism, it is like a knot at the end of the balloon. It allows us to have the Spirit with us *always* as we strive to keep the commandments.

Despite receiving this important gift, some young Latter-day Saints tell me, "I've never felt the Spirit." These young people have grown up in the Church and become so accustomed to having the Spirit with them, they take it for granted. They are like fish swimming around saying, "Water? What water? I don't see any water." Fish don't notice the water until they are out of it. Then they realize they were surrounded all along. Sadly, many young Latter-day Saints don't realize they were surrounded with the Spirit until, because of their poor choices, they distance themselves from Him. Then the difference becomes obvious.

One young woman said, "But, Brother Wilcox, everyone talks about feeling the Spirit in dramatic ways, and that has never happened in my life."

I responded, "We sing, 'The Spirit of God like a fire is burning' (*Hymns*, no. 2), and I have felt that fire, but not all the time. Sometimes the Spirit is more like a furnace."

If I came home and found my house on fire, I would notice. But when I come home on a cold day and enter my house, I don't usually say, "Oh, good, the furnace is working." I just go about my life feeling comfortable and happy. If I notice the furnace at all, it is when it is *not* working. Then I take steps quickly to correct the problem. It's the same with the Spirit. I said to the young woman, "Instead of looking back and feeling shortchanged because you have not felt the Spirit more powerfully, think back on the darkness, loneliness, and discouragement you have felt when the Spirit hasn't been with you, and be grateful those occasions are not the norm."

WITNESS

The Holy Ghost "witnesses of the Father and the Son" (2 Nephi 31:18) and reveals the "truth of all things" (Moroni 10:5). Through the Spirit we can receive a testimony that carries more certainty than knowledge received through our physical senses.

While our family served in Chile we met a wonderful sister, Maria Angelica, who was completely blind. She lived with her grown children, but she was the only one interested in learning about the Church. As soon as Maria Angelica began meeting with the missionaries, they asked my wife and me to pick her up for church meetings since she lived in our ward boundaries and had no other way of attending. Each Sunday when I helped her into our van, I would describe whatever tie I happened to be wearing and tell her how handsome I looked, since she was the only person I knew who couldn't contradict me.

During the week, members volunteered to join the elders at Maria Angelica's apartment and read to her from the Book of Mormon. We also arranged to get her the Book of Mormon on CD so she could listen on her own. When the missionaries asked how she felt about the book, she held it close to her heart and said, "Elders, I do not need to see it to know it's true."

After the Santiago Chile Temple was remodeled and before it was rededicated, there was an open house during which guests were escorted through in small groups. We made special

THE SPIRIT: MESSENGER OF GRACE

arrangements for Maria Angelica to have her own tour so she could experience the temple in her way. My wife and I joined the missionaries and helped this sweet investigator from room to room, where she had been given permission to touch everything. She felt the sculpted carpet, the legs of the tables and chairs, and the handcrafted door handles. She was thrilled to discover what I had not even noticed: the national flower of Chile, the *copihue*, was carved into all the door handles and on the woodwork of the chairs in the sealing rooms. She cried as she brushed her hands across the tops of altars where families could be united forever. As we watched her, we were moved deeply by how clearly she "saw" the temple.

Shortly after that tour, Maria Angelica committed to baptism. Later, as her children recognized the positive changes in their mother's life, they were also baptized. When our mission ended and it was time for us to leave Chile, Maria Angelica said to me, "President Wilcox, I know two things for sure. First, you are not as handsome as you think you are, and second, I know God and Jesus live and direct this Church." She did not need to see to know. The Spirit testified truth to her spirit.

President Joseph Fielding Smith taught, "When a man has the manifestation from the Holy Ghost, it leaves an indelible impression on his soul, one that is not easily erased. It is Spirit speaking to spirit, and it comes with convincing force. A manifestation of an angel or even the Son of God himself, would impress the eye and mind, and eventually become dimmed, but the impressions of the Holy Ghost sink deeper into the soul and are more difficult to erase."4

Surely a visitation by an angel would be accompanied by the Spirit, but even Alma, who saw an angel, said, "I testify unto you that I do know that these things whereof I have spoken are true. And how do ye suppose that I know of their surety? Behold, I say unto you they are made known unto me by the Holy Spirit of God" (Alma 5:45–46). The Spirit testifying to our spirits is a manifestation of grace. It is an infusion of divine help that enables us to draw closer to God and become more like Him.

COMFORTER

In addition to acting as a witness, the Holy Ghost is also a comforter. When children cry, they can usually be soothed by their parents' loving voices. In the same way, our spirits recognize the comforting voice of the Holy Ghost as it calms our fears and fills us "with hope and perfect love" (Moroni 8:26).

Our spirits recognize the comforting voice of the Holy Ghost as it calms our fears and fills us "with hope and perfect love" (Moroni 8:26).

When my daughter was little, she would sing "I Am a Child of God" (*Hymns,* no. 301), but instead of singing, "Lead me, guide me, walk beside me," she would sing, "Lead me, guide me, rock-a-bye me." Truly the Spirit allows us to feel "rock-a-byed" in times of distress.

I will always be grateful for the comfort I felt when my father, Ray T. Wilcox, passed away. He had a debilitating stroke that left him unable to speak or move. Once it was determined that nothing more could be done for him at the hospital, we brought him home and family members took turns caring for him. Before long, he slipped into a state of unconsciousness. The night he passed away, my son Russell and I were on duty. I took the first shift while Russell slept on the couch in the family room. I noticed Dad's breathing became labored and sporadic, and I knew the end was near. I sat on the edge of his bed and took his hand in mine. I hoped he knew he was not alone. When he finally took his last breath, all I could do was pray and thank God for my wonderful father.

When I was a child the whole idea of death frightened me. The thought of ever being with a dead body was terrifying. I guess I had seen too many scary movies or heard too many ghost stories. Yet, as I sat there with my father in the moments after his passing, I felt nothing but peace. The Spirit comforted me. My parents' bedroom window framed a view of the Provo Utah Temple across the valley from where they lived. As I looked at the temple lights that night, I was overwhelmed with gratitude for the Savior, the gospel, the temple, and the Spirit.

I then woke Russell and we called my brothers and their

wives. We decided not to wake Mom until everyone had gathered. Once we were all there, we circled Mom's bed, woke her, and told her Dad had passed away. She also felt the comfort of the Spirit as she nodded her head gently and said, "All is well! All is well!" (*Hymns*, no. 30).

Jesus told His disciples that when He could no longer be with them, He would send "the Comforter, which is the Holy Ghost." He promised, "Peace I leave with you, my peace I give unto you: not as the world giveth, give I unto you. Let not your heart be troubled, neither let it be afraid" (John 14:26–27). My family felt that peace when Dad passed. The comfort of the Spirit is a manifestation of grace, and it is one more way God can shape and change us.

GUIDE

Just as the Spirit can testify to us and comfort us, He can also guide us as we make important decisions. Corrina Carter, a young lady from St. George, Utah, told me about her uncle, Fernando Gonzales, who was in a rehabilitation center to overcome addictions. He was being taught he had to acknowledge a higher power in his life. The counselors took him out to a large corral, blindfolded him, and instructed him to find the horse. He had heard other participants talk of this exercise and thought he had figured out a way to beat the system. He brought an apple in his pocket, which he pulled out the minute he was

THE SPIRIT: MESSENGER OF GRACE

blindfolded. He thought the horse would come to him to get the apple and was feeling pretty smug about his brilliant plan—until he had wandered around the corral for what seemed like forever holding out an apple. The horse never came. He thought he was so smart, but all he had done was provide a good laugh to the staff members who were watching. He felt completely helpless. How was he supposed to find the horse, let alone harness it as he had been instructed to do? It seemed impossible. Fernando felt totally stupid, lost, and forsaken.

Then he felt someone touching his shoulder. It was another participant, who had been sent to help but was not allowed to speak. Fernando figured out that the other participant's taps were guiding him, and he finally found the horse and harnessed it. Only then was he allowed to take off his blindfold. His leaders gathered around him and told him this lesson was to teach him to stop thinking he could control everything and to depend instead on a higher power.

Fernando asked, "Okay, but if God is up in heaven, how does He touch my shoulder?"

Then someone remarked, "Come on, dude, this is Utah. Didn't you grow up in the Mormon Church? The one tapping you on the shoulder is like the Holy Ghost!" Suddenly all the Primary lessons from Fernando's childhood came flooding back, and everything made sense. He had once walked with God, but mortality was a time away from Him. The veil was his blindfold, but God could still lead him through the Spirit. Fernando said, "It was quite a spiritual moment for me." We read in Proverbs 3:5–6, "Trust in the Lord with all thine heart; and lean not unto thine own understanding. In all thy ways acknowledge him, and he shall direct thy paths."

For Corrina's uncle, the Holy Ghost was like someone tapping on his shoulder. To me, the Spirit's direction is like following a spiritual traffic light. When I speak to the youth, I teach them that after they make a decision they may feel a "stupor of thought" (D&C 9:9) restraining them. "That is like a red light," I say. Then I explain that sometimes after they make a decision they may feel a warm feeling—a confirming assurance of the Spirit that they are doing the right thing (see D&C 9:8). I tell them, "That is a green light."

Just like when we are driving, we get into a mess if we go forward on a red light or stop on a green. Of course, traffic signals change frequently, and sometimes the Spirit will change His directions as well. Most of us know what to do when we see a green or red light. We can even deal with a change in direction as long as the message is clear. The problem is the yellow lights. What do we do when we study things out in our minds, make a decision, take it to God as scriptures instruct, and get no response? That is a yellow light. When we are feeling neither a burning nor a stupor, we must proceed—with caution, of course—but proceed all the same.

THE SPIRIT: MESSENGER OF GRACE

Elder Richard G. Scott taught, "When we explain a problem and a proposed solution [to Heavenly Father], sometimes He answers yes, sometimes no. Often He withholds an answer, not for lack of concern, but because He loves us—perfectly. He wants us to apply truths He has given us. For us to grow, we need to trust our ability to make correct decisions."[5]

Some people become discouraged when they receive yellow lights. They assume it is evidence that God doesn't care or that He is too busy for them. I try to take the opposite point of view and see yellow lights as evidence that God trusts me. He knows I have made correct decisions in the past, and He trusts me to do it again. To me it seems like a vote of confidence that He doesn't feel He needs to direct my every move. We were sent to earth to obtain experience and develop faith. That purpose would be frustrated if the Spirit gave direction immediately for every decision. Elder Dallin H. Oaks taught, "We should study things out in our minds using the reasoning powers our Creator has placed within us. Then we should pray for guidance and act upon it if we receive it; if we do not receive guidance, we should act upon our best judgment."[6]

When we are feeling neither a burning nor a stupor, we must proceed—with caution, of course—but proceed all the same.

When I receive a yellow light, I proceed with faith and trust that if I really am about to mess up, God will stop me. I take comfort in the words Elder John H. Groberg once spoke to students at BYU: "Because [the Lord] knows we need growth, he generally does not point and say [the clear direction]. But if [a decision] is wrong, he will let us know—we will feel it for sure. I am positive of that. So rather than saying, 'I will not move until I have this burning in my heart,' let us turn it around and say, 'I will move unless I feel it is wrong.'"[7] The Spirit's guidance and direction is a manifestation of grace—an expression of divine help. It is one more way God draws us to Him and teaches us to be more like Him.

SANCTIFIER

Grace is evident in the Spirit's roles as witness, comforter, and guide, but perhaps it is in His role as sanctifier that we see grace most clearly. Through the Spirit we can be sanctified as we repent, receive ordinances, and remain true to our covenants (see Mosiah 5:1–6; 3 Nephi 27:20). "A redeemed man is a man who has partaken of the powers of Christ through the Atonement, repented of his sins, and been renewed through the Sanctifier, who is the Holy Ghost. The Holy Ghost is the midwife of salvation. He is the agent of the new birth, the sacred channel and power by which men and women are changed and renewed."[8]

Two young missionaries met a professor who had received

THE SPIRIT: MESSENGER OF GRACE

his credentials from Heidelberg University in Germany. They attempted to teach him, but his mind was far from open to their message. He wondered, *What could these two young kids who have not even graduated from college ever teach me?* The professor's wife seemed interested, but when the elders tried to set a return appointment, the man refused.

Not long after, the professor discovered he had to have a major surgery. While he was recuperating in the hospital, his yard and garden suffered. The two missionaries took it upon themselves to mow the lawn, trim the hedges, and weed the flowers.

When the wife told her husband what the missionaries had done, the professor sent for the elders to come to the hospital. He actually fought back his emotions as he said, "Never in my entire adult life has anyone ever gone out of his way to do anything like that for me." The act of service softened his heart, and he invited the missionaries to share their message. This time he set aside his pride and skepticism and listened to the lessons with new ears. Each time he and his wife met with the missionaries, he was visibly changed.

When the missionaries first asked him to pray, he refused. He said, "I prayed as a child, but I have long since given that practice up." Now he was more meek and humble. He agreed to pray, and not long after, he received a testimony and was baptized along with his wife.

Had the hospital stay changed the man's demeanor? Had the missionaries' service made him feel guilty for rejecting them? Did the man decide to listen in an attempt to please his wife? People may come up with many explanations for the man's change of heart, but in reality it was the Spirit that had touched him and begun to sanctify him.[9]

To share a more personal example, I first met Hal Jones shortly after he and his wife, Barbara, had joined the Church. He owned a successful road construction company in California and was a tough, hard-nosed businessman. He and Barbara first came in contact with the Church when they visited Temple Square. They had a layover in Salt Lake City, and Hal suggested they go see the Mormon Temple. Barbara, a faithful Catholic, refused. Hal said, "Think of it as a historical monument," and off they went.

During the visit, Barbara had a very spiritual experience. When the sister missionaries passed the couple a card and asked if they wanted to be visited at their home, Hal said, "Be sure to mark no." Barbara marked yes, and the rest is history. Hal and Barbara and their two children were baptized. Of course, Hal said he was only doing it for his kids. He looked at the Church like he did the Boy Scouts—a good organization for the youth. He paid tithing and quit drinking but considered these sacrifices the dues he paid to be part of a great club. It was obvious he was still pretty rough around the edges when he was asked to share his testimony shortly after his baptism and announced in a loud voice, "The Mormon Church is the best @#*$ thing to ever happen to America!"

Over the years I watched his crusty personality soften. I saw his motives change. He may have started out in the Church for his children, but soon he realized it was making a difference in his own life, too. He began to express love more consistently to his wife, and they enjoyed a closer marriage. I watched him become more refined, generous, and tender. He was often touched to the point of tears when he heard missionaries report their missions or young people share their experiences at Especially for Youth or youth conference. This important businessman—whose spare time had previously been spent playing handball or golf—now made time to go home teaching and read the *Ensign* each month. He loved attending general conference. Slowly but surely the layers of the old Hal began to fall away, revealing a new Hal in his place.

Hal valued education. When I was teaching elementary school, he encouraged me to get my master's degree, which I did. Next he prodded me to earn my doctorate. I remember sitting at a restaurant with a group of friends when Hal asked if I had applied to any doctoral programs. I just smiled and said, "Hey, I just finished my master's degree. I need a break."

Later that evening Hal pulled me aside privately and pushed me again to apply. I explained, "Hal, I have to be honest with you. Debi and I have four kids, and we are living on my teaching salary and the paycheck my wife brings home from working a few days a week as a nurse. I don't have the money for a doctorate."

I will never forget how selflessly he replied, "Money? Is that all that is holding you back? For goodness' sake, Brad, I have money! I will help you pay for school." And, true to his word, he did.

When Hal passed away, Debi and I attended his viewing and funeral. I stood before Hal's body, which was dressed in his white temple clothes, and marveled at how he had been sanctified through the years. I saw firsthand how the Spirit had changed this hard-shelled, tough-talking road builder into a godly man. The change didn't happen overnight, but it happened. In the New Testament, Paul wrote, "If any man be in Christ, he is a new creature: old things are passed away; behold, all things are become new" (2 Corinthians 5:17). As surely as a caterpillar turns into a butterfly, I saw Hal Jones become a new creature in Christ.

We all stand in awe of Captain Moroni. The Book of Mormon says, "If all men had been, and were, and ever would be, like unto Moroni, behold, the very powers of hell would

The change didn't happen overnight, but it happened.

THE SPIRIT: MESSENGER OF GRACE

have been shaken forever" (Alma 48:17). But Moroni did not start out that way. He also had to be sanctified by the Holy Ghost. My friend Joe Cochran, who speaks often to the youth, pointed out to me that in the next verse we are told that Captain Moroni "was a man like unto Ammon, the son of Mosiah, yea, and even the other sons of Mosiah, yea, and also Alma and his sons, for they were all men of God" (Alma 48:18).

Men of God? Remember that at one point Alma and the sons of Mosiah were "numbered among the unbelievers" and went "about secretly . . . seeking to destroy the church, and to lead astray the people of the Lord" (Mosiah 27:8, 10). Yet later we read they were men of God like Captain Moroni. One of the sons of Alma was Corianton, who went home early from his mission due to his immorality (see Alma 39). Yet several chapters later we read that he was a man of God (see Alma 48:18; 43:1; 49:30). That is the miracle of grace! Through the sanctifying power of the Holy Ghost, those who appear to be bound for hell can become the very people who cause the powers of hell to shake. The sanctification of the Spirit is a manifestation of grace that enables us to change and become more like God. As it happened for Alma and the sons of Mosiah, it happened for the professor who joined the Church and happened for Hal Jones. As it happened for them, it can happen for us.

Remember that Elder Robert E. Wells spoke of the adventures of the Spirit—unforgettable experiences during which we see how intimately God is involved in our lives. These are the moments when we recognize the Holy Ghost as it witnesses, comforts, and guides us—moments when we receive grace from the messenger of grace and are sanctified. I'll leave jaguars, piranhas, and piloting airplanes to Elder Wells and his equally adventurous wife, Helen. I don't share their same spirit of adventure. But, like them, I could never give up the adventures of the Spirit. They are the ones that change us forever.

Chapter 5

ESCAPING BONDAGE

In the Book of Mormon, King Limhi's people were in bondage to the Lamanites: "And now the afflictions of the Nephites were great, and there was no way that they could deliver themselves out of their hands, for the Lamanites had surrounded them on every side" (Mosiah 21:5). Three times the Nephites went to battle against their enemies, and "the Lamanites did beat them, and drove them back, and slew many of them" (Mosiah 21:8).

It was only as the people of Limhi finally sought the Lord's grace that they were successful: "They did humble themselves even in the depths of humility; and they did cry mightily to God . . . that he would deliver them out of their afflictions" (Mosiah 21:14).

Sometimes our progress is blocked by bad habits and

addictions, and we feel like we are in bondage. When we or those we love are caught in negative cycles of compulsive behavior, we can turn to God, and with His help—His grace—we can escape. But one of the reasons I love the story of Limhi is because the happy ending doesn't come immediately after the people call upon God. Many who struggle with addictions relate to King Limhi's people, who spent "many days in the wilderness" before "they arrived in the land of Zarahemla" (Mosiah 22:13). But God and His grace were not waiting for them in Zarahemla. They were with them in the wilderness. Christ said, "I am the way" (John 14:6), not "I am waiting at the end of the way."

The miracle of grace is not just that God can take us out of slavery, but that He can take slavery out of us.

God cannot force us to choose the path of exaltation any more than He could force Limhi's people to leave their captivity. As hard as it is to comprehend, many are content with slavery. They either can't remember a past without it or can't imagine a future free from it. The miracle of grace is not just that God can take us out of slavery, but that He can take slavery out of us. It took weeks and months to bring the children of Israel out of Egypt. However, it took forty years and more to take Egypt out of them. It was one thing to change their surroundings and another to change them. As we strive to escape whatever bondage we find ourselves in, God will soften hearts, ease burdens (see Mosiah 21:15), and help us "grow in grace" (*Hymns,* no. 296; D&C 50:40). As we endure, we will learn to take the Lord's name more sincerely and reach out to others for help. We will learn to see our progress—however slow it may be—with a long-term perspective. When we choose to accept grace, our days in the wilderness—like those of Limhi—become journeys of freedom and healing.

ENDURE

My daughter Wendee and son-in-law Gian are trying to teach their son to write the alphabet. He tries, but he becomes easily discouraged because his letters are squiggly and uneven. They don't look like the ones his parents make, so he quickly gives up. He doesn't realize that his mom and dad don't care what the letters look like at this point, only that he keeps trying. They just want him to show a willing attitude.

One young man told me, "There is no chance for me. I have gone too far too often. I have let God down too many times. I am not worthy of His love or help." This young man was discouraged because he would make progress for a while, feel better, and then slip and decide all his efforts meant nothing.

Sometimes our growth and progress are like a game my friends and I would play on long bus rides home from debate trips in high school. It was called Matthew, Mark, Luke, and

John. Without breaking the rhythm of slapping our knees and clapping our hands, we had to call out someone else's name or number. Anyone who made a mistake had to go to the back of the bus and slowly start moving toward the front again, one seat at a time. Inevitably, when I had almost made it to the front, I would mess up and get sent to the back. I felt like I was getting nowhere. What I realize now is that no matter where I was sitting, the bus was still continually taking me toward home.

Enduring to the end doesn't mean living without errors. It means enduring in the covenant despite errors—remaining in the bus and continuing to play the game no matter where we currently sit or how many times we end up at the back.

When we feel discouraged, we can think of the text of the hymn "We Thank Thee, O God, for a Prophet": "Thus on to eternal perfection the honest and faithful will go" (*Hymns*, no. 19). Notice it says honest and faithful, not flawless and faultless. Worthiness is not flawlessness. It is honesty with self, God, and priesthood leaders. It is faithfully continuing to try. Scriptures promise our confidence will "wax strong in the presence of God" when we "let virtue garnish [our] thoughts unceasingly" (D&C 121:45). Such perfection is a great goal to strive for, but in the meantime, those who are honest with priesthood leaders and who keep trying can also feel their confidence wax strong.

A young woman in my mission prep class at BYU wrote me this e-mail: "I kept having feelings that I was not worthy enough to go on a mission. You said to get 'everything out on the table' in our interviews. That gave me the courage to finally talk to my bishop about some things from my past—weight that I have been carrying for a long time. [Since] I spoke to him I have never felt so free and so worthy. It took a lot of faith and humility to admit my own imperfections and admit I needed a Savior. But now I can go on my mission with complete confidence. I feel ready and worthy to enter the temple and most important, I know that if I slip up again, I am not going to hide it. I am going straight to my bishop or mission president."

Elder Jeffrey R. Holland reminded us to keep trying even when our successes can only be measured in "small victories."[1] He said, "The Lord blesses those who *want* to improve, who accept the need for commandments, and *try* to keep them. . . . If you stumble in that pursuit, so does everyone; the Savior is there to help you keep going."[2]

THE LORD'S NAME

King Limhi and his people tried to escape on their own without success. As they humbly turned to God, the result was different. In scriptures we are commanded, "Thou shalt not take the name of the Lord thy God in vain" (Exodus 20:7). Obviously this means we should not swear using the name of the Lord. However, refusing to take the Lord's name in vain has other meanings as well.

Taylor Halverson, who works in BYU's Center for Teaching and Learning, told me that the Hebrew word that was translated in our scriptures as *vain* means "meaningless and empty." He said, "Perhaps the commandment in Exodus 20:7 should read, 'Thou shalt not take upon thyself the name of God with empty and meaningless intent.'"[3] As we partake of the sacrament, we renew a covenant to take Christ's name upon us, just as Christ took our names upon Himself when He atoned for us. When we renew this covenant out of habit rather than as a sincere choice, we are taking His name in vain. The good news is we are familiar with the sacrament hymns and prayers. The bad news is we are familiar with the sacrament hymns and prayers.

Another way we take the Lord's name in vain is when we give up the hope Christ offers through His Atonement. In that moment, we render His grace useless, empty, and meaningless in our lives. In sacred sacrament moments, we cannot really promise to never again make a mistake. Instead we demonstrate that we are *willing* to receive His grace (see Moroni 4:3; D&C 46:9; emphasis added). If we abstain from taking the sacrament when we have not been specifically instructed to do so, we are choosing to look backward rather than forward. We are letting our yesterdays eat up too much of our todays and tomorrows.

Elder John H. Groberg taught, "What does it mean to partake of the sacrament worthily? Or how do we know if we are unworthy? If we *desire* to improve (which is to repent) and are not under priesthood restriction, then . . . we are worthy."[4] But what if we are under priesthood restriction? Is that taking away the very thing we need most? No. The restriction of sacrament privileges is not a punishment as much as it is an opportunity for us to stop and think seriously about what we're doing and our true desires. It is a chance to make sure we're not taking Christ's name and renewing covenants in an empty and meaningless way (see 3 Nephi 18:29–32).

One Easter I was invited to speak to women who lived in a halfway house in Salt Lake City. Many were members of the Church or former members who were desirous to participate in meetings. Since their travel was restricted, the local stake organized a small branch for them that met in a nearby seminary building.

As I drove into the small parking lot, I saw a group of about ten women outside the seminary building smoking before they entered sacrament meeting. They were embarrassed that I had seen them, so when I stood to speak I tried to ease the awkwardness of the moment by saying: "Thank you for choosing to be here. Too many people let those stupid cigarettes keep them from attending services like this, but Easter is not just about Christ breaking the bands of death. It is about His willingness to help us break bad habits." That meeting will always be a treasured memory—not in spite of the smell of smoke, but because of it.

Those women did not have to be there. Attendance was not required. They could have found many excuses for not going. Yet there they were. At the end of the meeting I greeted the sisters as they left. One woman whispered, "I had convinced myself that the Atonement could never apply to me, but now I know it does." As that sister shook my hand, I could tell she had not taken the sacrament meaninglessly that day. She had renewed her covenant to take upon herself the name of Christ, and she did not take His name in vain. She felt His grace.

REACH OUT

We do not need to try to escape bondage on our own. I'm sure it was easier for Limhi and his people to escape because they were working together. We can reach out to family members, friends, priesthood leaders, and professionals for help. The simple act of sharing with other people a desire—even a spark of a desire—to break bad habits dramatically increases the likelihood of success.

Being stuck in bad habits is like being stuck in quicksand. I've seen quicksand only in the movies, but my son-in-law Landon tells me the movies portray it pretty inaccurately. Apparently people don't typically drown in quicksand. When they die, it is from exposure or thirst because they are alone. It turns out the real danger of quicksand is encountering it when no one is around. People simply cannot get out without assistance. The more they try on their own, the more stuck they become. Survivors are those who call out for and accept help from others.

Hiding and attempting to cover our problems can be as damaging as the problems themselves. One man who was heavily involved in pornography didn't want anyone to find out. He said, "I stopped praying because I felt hypocritical. I didn't tell my bishop or anyone in my family. I determined that all I needed was willpower and promised myself that once I conquered my weakness on my own, I would again pray and speak openly with my bishop and wife." Such thinking seems like someone stuck in quicksand saying, "Once I take care of this on my own, I will let others know what happened."

Survivors are those who call out for and accept help from others.

There is wisdom in building a support system—a circle of examples, mentors, and friends intent on encouraging instead of shaming, educating instead of embarrassing. As I travel I meet hundreds of facilitators and missionaries who serve in the Church's Addiction Recovery Program. How I love and admire these faithful brothers and sisters.

They help people identify and remove stumbling blocks. We're familiar with the advice given in Matthew 5:30—"If thy right hand offend thee, cut it off"—yet we are unclear what that statement really means. The original Greek word that was translated as *offend* could also have been translated as "cause to stumble." In other words, if our hand is tempted to touch something that would cause us to stumble spiritually, the Savior's advice is to get rid of the temptation, cut it out of our lives completely. A support system can help us do that.

> "Never again" may be where we want to end up, but it is not where we start.

Priesthood leaders can be part of that circle of support. Latter-day Saints are not the only ones who see value in confessing sins, but many Christians confess anonymously. We speak with priesthood leaders face to face. That way, along with hearing our confessions, they can help us set realistic goals and hold us accountable as we strive to reach them.

A series of small, specific goals is often better than one big, nebulous goal. "Never again" may be where we want to end up, but it is not where we start. Start with a day, and then a week, then two. President Henry B. Eyring suggested, "We can have rising expectations. You can set the bar for yourself a little higher and then a little higher, again and again."[5]

Leaders and others who support us can help us celebrate private victories. When kids mow the lawn or set the table without being asked, we say, "Wonderful!" This reinforcement gives them enthusiasm to keep making the same positive choices again. But what happens when we resist temptation? Usually no one knows but us. That changes when we share our victories with others who can join with us in celebrating important milestones.

When we don't succeed, mentors and friends can help us learn from mistakes. Although we don't seek, plan, or condone mistakes, they are part of life and part of any effort toward self-betterment. Mentors can help us reflect on our choices, figure out what caused us to backslide, and find renewed motivation. A lapse does not have to become a relapse. Satan would have us dwell on our mistakes and wallow around in self-pity. Leaders can help us to examine our failures, determine what led to the poor choice, and figure out what we can do in the future when confronted with the same situation.

LONG-TERM PERSPECTIVE

God saw the journey of Limhi and his people differently than they did. Remember when your aunt or uncle would see you at a family reunion and say, "You are growing like a weed. I can't believe how much you have changed"? You never noticed the growth as you looked in the mirror each day, but your loving family members had a long-term perspective. God has an eternal perspective. Where we see death, He sees a homecoming. Where we see suffering, He sees growth. Where we see failures, He sees the road to success.

Once I was in a public school doing a demonstration lesson for BYU student teachers. I was scheduled to teach the second-graders as the future teachers observed. No sooner had I begun than one of the children screamed, "He's coming!" and the class jumped out of their seats and ran to a table at the side of the room. I looked at the regular classroom teacher, who felt embarrassed and quickly explained that they were hatching chicks in an incubator. One of the children had noticed that a chick had begun to break through its shell, and the children could not contain their excitement.

The adults gathered behind the second-graders to watch the miracle of life unfold. The children watched as the little chick pushed and pecked against the shell, which stubbornly refused to give way. After a while, one second-grader looked up at me and said, "Mr. Wilcox, help him! Can't you see he's having a hard time?"

I have to admit it was tempting. For two seconds I considered reaching into the incubator and cracking open the egg so the children would be willing to return to their seats and we could get on with the lesson. However, I knew that cracking open that egg would not have helped the chick. It probably would have killed it, for only as the chick pushes against the shell does it gain the strength to survive outside the shell.

Breaking bad habits takes time, but each small goal reached along the way is how God strengthens us so we can maintain the needed changes in the long run. If the process were easier we would surely be disappointed in the outcome. The second-graders and I had to be patient and adopt a long-term perspective. We all do. When our vision is expanded by Him whose vision is perfect, it is evidence of God's grace.

One missionary needed to leave his mission a month early in order to accept a job awaiting him at home. His mission president understood the situation and told him he would make the arrangements. Still the elder was tormented by guilt. He wrote me an e-mail seeking advice: "Am I doing the right thing? I love the Savior and don't want to disappoint Him, but this is an incredible work opportunity. I am just so torn."

I wrote back, "Keep a long-term perspective! God is guiding you through a perfecting process that is longer than your mission. He is in it for the long haul. You are not shortchanging Him by a month. You are just twenty-three months into a mission that is going to continue throughout your life and beyond."

When my son David was teaching Japanese at the MTC, one of the missionaries in his district became pretty stressed out. The young man said, "I want to be able to look back and say I did all I could to accomplish my purpose and reach my potential. This is the only time I will ever have to do this, and I don't want to spend forever wondering if there was more I could have done. I feel like what happens right now will determine the rest of my life and even stretches into where I will end up eternally. It really scares me to think that I might—and probably will—screw up. There is so much riding on this one single moment, it's ridiculous."

David told him, "Are missions important? Yes. Do the lessons learned on missions affect the future? Yes. Do missionaries screw up? Yes, but let's keep things in perspective. Imagine a first-grader saying the same words: I want to be able to look back at first grade and say I did all I could do. This is the only time I will ever be in first grade. What happens right now will determine my future. It scares me that I might make a mistake."

When David put it in those terms, the stressed-out elder just laughed. What would we say to that first-grader? We would probably say, "Hey, don't freak out. There is a second-grade teacher waiting who knows exactly how to help you get to the next step. Your future is not determined by first grade alone. Don't be afraid of mistakes. We all make them as we learn."

JOURNEY OF HEALING

As we read of the escape of Limhi and his people, we often think it was only a journey toward freedom, but it was also a journey of healing. Freedom in the future always requires healing from the past. The Lord's grace offered Limhi's people both, and He offers the same to us.

ESCAPING BONDAGE

Stephen was introduced to pornography when he was twelve. He said, "The rush I felt was strong and powerful, but I knew it was wrong so I quickly tried to stop. I had no clue about the devastation and heartache that porn would bring into my life. I had no idea I would become an addict."

Throughout his youth, Stephen appeared to be a good Mormon kid—saying his prayers, reading scriptures, and going to church. But he said, "I was doing Christlike things without becoming Christlike. Privately I was fighting a constant battle against temptation. Sometimes I had weeks and months of sobriety, but usually it lasted only a few days."

> *Freedom in the future always requires healing from the past.*

Stephen convinced himself that his private actions didn't hurt others and he could handle it alone. He kept telling himself it wasn't a big problem. "Besides," he reasoned, "it's not holding me back in school or in other aspects of my life, so it can't be all that bad."

Soon enough, his private indulgences did start affecting other aspects of his life—especially his spirituality. He said, "I stopped praying because I felt unworthy to approach God. I avoided the bishop because I was afraid he would ask me about it. I stopped trying to repent since I always fell again. I had been taught that I wouldn't get God's approval and grace until

I worked as hard as I could first, and in my mind that meant breaking my bad habits once and for all. Repenting and falling again felt like I was mocking the Atonement. It seemed better to put off repentance until I was finally done. That reasoning just kept me away from God when I needed Him most."

As the time for Stephen's mission drew closer, social pressure gave him enough motivation to clean up his act and serve. He was grateful for that reprieve in his life. However, it did not lead to lasting change. He said, "There is a big difference between not viewing because you are making a conscious choice and not viewing because you simply don't have the opportunity. It's like going on a diet instead of making permanent lifestyle changes."

After his mission, Stephen met McKenna, and they were married in the temple. They were happy, and Stephen felt that now that he had a sexual outlet, he would no longer feel tempted to view pornography. He learned quickly that marriage is not a cure. Those who struggle to control themselves outside of marriage continue to struggle within marriage. Stephen underestimated the depth of his youthful addiction. Six months after his wedding, pornography crept back into his life. "At that point, I gave up trying. I went to church and partook of the sacrament, but it meant nothing to me," he explained.

When people asked him how marriage was or how he was doing, he would answer, "Everything is great." He said it so often he actually started to believe it. He said, "I was being pacified and lulled by Satan, just as we are warned in scriptures." In 2 Nephi 28:21 we read, "And others will he pacify, and lull them away into carnal security, that they will say: All is well . . . and thus the devil cheateth their souls."

The material for the Addiction Recovery Program states, "Individuals finally become willing to abstain when the pain of the problem becomes worse than the pain of the solution."[6]

That was what finally happened in Stephen's life. He explained, "My addiction became progressively worse until I was completely out of control. I was viewing and acting out daily—even multiple times a day. Our first child had just been born a few months earlier, and I should have been so happy. Instead, I was miserable. I no longer cared who found out. I knew I could lose my wife, my son, everything, but I could not go on the way I was. I finally reached out for help." The material used in the Addiction Recovery Program calls it hitting bottom. After years of hiding and justifying, that's what happened to Stephen.

He disclosed everything to McKenna, who was devastated. "Her response made me realize how far off track I had allowed myself to become," Steven admitted. "I was sick. I let my life get so out of control. I was angry—not at my wife or because I told her. She deserved to know the truth. I was angry at myself for being such an idiot." Stephen began the repentance process.

He spoke to his bishop and began participating in Addiction Recovery.

President Thomas S. Monson said, "May we ever choose the harder right instead of the easier wrong."[7] Stephen had been taking the easy path by sweeping his problem under the rug and telling himself it was no big deal—that everybody did it and that lots of people say it is normal and even healthy.

"The problem with the easy road," said Stephen, "is that it did not lead me where I wanted to be. It left me weaker rather than stronger for traveling it. If pornography is so normal and healthy, why was I so unhappy and why was my life falling apart?" Now Stephen chose a harder road. It was grace that helped him face the issue head-on, reach out for help, learn the facts, and honestly own up to his actions. It was a hard road, but he knew that now he was getting somewhere. That was the long-term perspective he had been missing.

McKenna faced a difficult journey of her own. She said, "April 15, 2011, was a day I will never forget because it was the day my whole world crumbled around me. I grew up in the Church and graduated from seminary. I went to BYU and got married in the temple. My life seemed perfect. Suddenly everything changed."

Three months after their first baby, a son, was born, Stephen told her everything he had been hiding. She said, "My husband, my sweetheart, the man I loved with my whole heart, the man

ESCAPING BONDAGE

I had married in the temple for eternity, and with whom I just started a family, was a porn addict. I never thought something like that could happen to me." She admitted she had seen warning signs and knew things weren't quite right, but she had been afraid to confront her husband. She had enough on her plate dealing with the pregnancy, delivery, and new baby. She said, "Looking back, I can see that I was receiving strong promptings from the Holy Ghost, but I disregarded them and kept pretending everything was fine. I was in denial. My husband was in the bondage of pornography, but I was in bondage as well—the bondage of ignorance."

Elder Jeffrey R. Holland wrote, "We learn little clichés early in our lives. Two of them are 'Ignorance is bliss' and 'What I don't know won't hurt me.' Let me say with all the intensity I have that nothing will hurt you *more* than what you don't know."[8]

McKenna learned the truth of those words. She said, "Stephen's disclosure hit me like a tidal wave of despair, a tsunami of the soul. The first few days were full of grief, anger, frustration, and disbelief. I was recovering from the birth and caring for my newborn. On top of that I was dealing with my husband's confession. I felt rejected and guilty for not being enough for him. I felt lost, alone, full of shame, and beyond the reach of anyone or anything."

She asked for God's help and was prompted to attend a

spouse support meeting held in conjunction with Stephen's Addiction Recovery Group. As others shared their experiences at the meeting, McKenna realized she was not alone. She said, "I couldn't listen hard enough, write notes fast enough, or absorb quickly enough. I started attending to try to understand my husband, but then I stayed for me."

McKenna realized that she needed the Savior's grace just as Stephen did. They both needed strength and help. The Atonement is not just about her husband receiving forgiveness but also about helping her to forgive. The Atonement is about helping both of them heal. McKenna said, "I came to understand that no matter what Stephen's choices were, the Savior would help me find the peace and joy that I so desperately needed." Stephen's choices had affected her, but it wasn't her husband's responsibility to change so she could feel better. She had to be responsible for her own feelings.

Both Stephen and McKenna found that help from heaven came to them like manna came to the Israelites—just enough to sustain them from one day to the next (see Exodus 16:23–30). McKenna said, "God would give me just enough peace, courage, and strength to get through one day at a time."

McKenna had always prayed, but never before with such intensity. She said, "I knew God was the only one who could get us out of this mess. Once when my son was three months old I was rocking him because he was crying, and then suddenly I was crying too. In an attempt to calm both of us, I sang, 'Heavenly Father, are you really there? And do you hear and answer every child's prayer?' (*Children's Songbook*, 12). I wasn't just singing a song. I was asking those questions in earnest. I needed to know if God was really there and if He cared. Peace came, and also the realization that if I truly knew those things, my testimony needed to be reflected in my behavior. I needed to make some changes." She renewed her efforts to read the scriptures—even a few verses at a time—and draw closer to God. In time she started seeing herself, her husband, and their situation through spiritual eyes. She said, "Grace changed my perspective. That change had to come from outside of me. I was too close to the situation to do it myself. New understandings opened the door for forgiveness and love."

Stephen felt grace sustaining him as he progressed as well. He explained, "Looking back, I can see the Lord's miracles began immediately, but it was difficult to see them clearly in the moment. First, I experienced the miracle of forgiveness. I was in an addiction recovery meeting and one of the missionaries testified that we could be forgiven. In that moment it was like the Savior wrapped His arms around me and the weight was lifted. Tears filled my eyes and rolled down my cheeks." Did that special feeling mean Stephen never messed up again? No. The miracle of forgiveness is not the once-and-for-all event Stephen had pictured when he was younger. Scriptures tell us to confess and forsake (see D&C 58:43), but forsaking is usually a process in which forgiveness is offered over and over again. When Stephen was younger, he thought he was mocking the Atonement by falling after feeling forgiven. "Now," he says, "I believe those who mock the Atonement are those who refuse to try at all."

Stephen also experienced the miracle of recovery. He said, "I used to define success as not acting out. Now I understand that true recovery is a change of heart. It's not about external behavior alone, but what's inside. For fifteen years I gritted my teeth and tried to fix my problem on my own. Finally, I gave it to the Lord and am allowing Him to change my heart. My capacity has been increased. I now count many more victories than defeats."

Along with forgiveness and recovery, Stephen recognized the miracle of healing. "I was once so full of shame that I would rather have died than tell anyone about my problem. In less than a year the Lord worked such a miracle of healing in my heart that I am now able to share my experience with others as I try to help them. Whether it's one-on-one or in large groups,

> *Scriptures tell us to confess and forsake (see D&C 58:43), but forsaking is usually a process in which forgiveness is offered over and over again.*

I can speak openly and honestly about my past, and the toxic sting of guilt and shame is gone."

When Stephen speaks of miracles, he uses the word accurately. A miracle is an event that mortals can't cause to happen without God's intervention. The forgiveness, recovery, and healing that Stephen experienced are gifts from God and evidence of His grace. McKenna's peace and perspective are also gifts of grace. Grace has helped both of them.

Stephen and McKenna are making it through this. Trust began to grow where once it had been destroyed. Love began to appear where once it had been leveled to the ground. They committed to communicating their physical and emotional needs to each other and being more sensitive to meeting those needs. They now have three young sons. They are the first to acknowledge they still face their share of challenges, but they face them together and with great faith.

Stephen shared, "My marriage never ended on paper, but it did in every other way. It was my fault. Logic would have said to scrap it and start over. Fortunately, because of our temple marriage, McKenna and I were not willing to give up, and the Lord never gave up on us. We are stronger and happier for it."

McKenna agreed, "I know I truly have a Redeemer, because He has redeemed my marriage. I am happier now than I was when we first got married. We love each other at a much deeper level. Only a living God could have breathed life back into my dead marriage. Our marriage today is proof that God lives and His grace is real."

Bondage comes in many forms. For Limhi's people it was the bondage of slavery. For many today, it is the bondage of addictions, selfishness, ignorance, and pride. Regardless of the type of bondage, the Savior's grace isn't *a* solution; it is *the* solution. It isn't *a* reason for hope; it is *the* reason. As we endure and take our covenants seriously, God will send people to help and allow us to see ourselves and our struggles through a long-term perspective. He will journey with us and grant deliverance, freedom, and healing.

"And after being many days in the wilderness" King Limhi and his people "arrived in the land of Zarahemla" and "Mosiah received them with joy" (Mosiah 22:13–14). It is with joy that our King will also receive us—not just at the end of our journey, but all along the way.

Chapter 6

"I KNOW IN WHOM I HAVE TRUSTED"

"When our twin daughters were young, [we] decided to teach them to swim," wrote Stephen E. Robinson. He knew he was helping his daughters, but from their perspective it seemed as if their dad were trying to drown them. One of his daughters was so frightened she began to scream, cry, kick, and scratch. She was completely unteachable.

Brother Robinson shared, "Finally, I held her close and said, 'Becky, I've got you. I'm your dad. I love you. I'm not going to let anything bad happen to you. Now relax.'" Slowly, she trusted him and began to relax in his arms. Then Brother Robinson put his arms under her and encouraged her to kick her legs, and pretty soon she was learning how to swim.

He wrote, "Spiritually, some of us are so terrified by the questions 'Am I celestial? Am I going to make it?' that we cannot make any progress. We're petrified by our fear. But if we're trying to follow his teachings and paying attention, we can almost feel the Savior's arms around us and feel those assurances as the Spirit whispers of the Savior's love for us: I love you. Trust me. And if we do trust him, he can begin to help us live the gospel."[1]

One definition of trust is *assured reliance*. In Mosiah 29:20 we read that the Lord works "with his power . . . among the children of men, extending the arm of mercy towards them that put their trust in him." Deep down we all know that trusting Jesus is the right answer, but it becomes difficult when other people have let us down.

Perhaps we have trusted people as Becky trusted her father in the swimming pool, but they have let us sink. When teachers, Church leaders, spouses, and other family members—the very ones who are supposed to have our best interests in mind—hurt us, we swear we will never trust again. We can't even trust ourselves, since we rarely live up to our own expectations. Others' failings, and our own, make us leery of trusting God. We fear exposing our inadequecies, becoming vulnerable, and getting hurt. The only way to open our hearts again is to better understand the facets or elements that make up trust and the sources that lead to mistrust. This allows us to trust God again as we once did in the premortal existence and paves the way for us to feel the newness of life His grace offers.

FACETS OF TRUST

Researchers in education have identified five facets of trust[2] that apply to trusting God's grace as well. For trust to exist there has to be benevolence—a high level of caring, positive intentions, and fairness—but also expressions of appreciation and love. To trust God we must believe He is benevolent (see Acts 10:34; 1 John 4:16).

Honesty is vital. Trust depends on integrity, truth, keeping promises, and avoiding manipulation. How can we have trust in God if we feel manipulated by Him? We must believe God is honest and cannot lie (see Titus 1:2; Ether 3:12).

The next facet of trust is openness, which includes shared decision-making and clear communication. We must believe that God allows us to make our own choices but also desires to maintain open communication with us about those choices through prayer (see Luke 21:36; 3 Nephi 18:15; D&C 20:33).

The final facets of trust are reliability and competence. When people are consistent, dependable, and committed, they open the door for trust. When they are capable, they seal the deal. Trustworthy people are positive examples and effective problem solvers. They know how to handle difficult situations when they come up. We must believe that God is fully reliable and competent but also flexible enough to help us handle anything that surfaces in our lives. We can be assured that God takes in stride whatever takes us by surprise.

When these five facets are in place, we are willing to trust God and His grace. With Isaiah we can declare, "I will trust, and not be afraid: for the Lord Jehovah is my strength and my song; he also is become my salvation" (Isaiah 12:2).

SOURCES OF MISTRUST

Sounds pretty straightforward, so why do we sometimes lack Isaiah's confidence? Often we guard ourselves and distance ourselves from God even when we know we need Him.

> *God takes in stride whatever takes us by surprise.*

I once had the opportunity to speak at BYU Women's Conference with Sister Kathleen H. Hughes, former member of the Relief Society general presidency. She spoke very openly with the sisters when she said, "When life becomes too busy, I sometimes fall short when it comes to letting go and trusting God and Christ. I become too stressed with the events of the day or week or month. I take it all on myself rather than turning it over to God."³ Even when we desire to "turn it over to God," we wonder what that means and how exactly to do it.

Let's go back to the idea of benevolence. We don't doubt God's benevolence as a general rule, but when we are confronted with life's unfairness or individual suffering, we can begin to wonder. When we pray for help and it doesn't seem to come, we become discouraged. Even with a knowledge of the plan of salvation, it is easy to feel like the rug gets pulled out from under us more often than we wish. Anger and bitterness can quickly replace trust if we let them. Even when things are going smoothly, it is easy to believe others are much more deserving of God's attention than we are. We know "God is love" (1 John 4:16), but we also know we are not always loveable. Peace comes when we remember that God sees more than mortality. He loves our pasts and futures as well as who we are now. Everything He does—even when it leaves us scratching our heads—is done with our best interests in mind (see 2 Nephi 26:33).

How about honesty? We know God is honest, but that knowledge can fill us with fear as easily as it fills us with peace. He can see beyond our flimsy facades and hypocritical masks. Fear must be replaced with faith—faith that He is honest when He tells us He brought us forth at this time for a purpose and has given us everything we need to succeed. God sees the real us. That also means that in His honesty, He sees good in us that we don't even see in ourselves.

And openness? God is willing to communicate. We know we should pray. We just don't always know how those prayers interact with God's will and others' agency. Even when answers come, they rarely come complete with explanations and instructions. In faith we seek priesthood blessings and hear promises uttered that are not immediately fulfilled. It may take us years to realize that some of the greatest evidences of God's love are the closed doors He sends when we are praying for open ones.

Reliability? Most of us agree that God is reliable and dependable, but our limited view makes us question His timing. We sing, "Jesus, Savior, pilot me" (*Hymns*, no. 104), but we still want to file our own flight plan and direct every takeoff and landing according to our schedule (see Helaman 12:6). God views all things—including time—differently than we do (see Alma 40:8). His delays are not always denials. If we can look back and see His hand in our lives in the past, we must press forward believing that same hand will be evident in the future. If we can see He has brought us to this point, we must believe He does not intend to drop us now.

If we can look back and see His hand in our lives in the past, we must press forward believing that same hand will be evident in the future.

Competence? We rarely mistrust God's ability. After all, He possesses all knowledge and power (see 1 Nephi 9:6). But that assurance doesn't keep us from assuming God is so busy helping everyone else that He doesn't have time for us. Since God is competent enough to have numberless children, we must believe He is competent enough to know and care for each of us individually. God comprehends what we cannot (see Mosiah 4:9). His charity never faileth (see Moroni

7:46; 1 Corinthians 13:8), and His strength is perfect (see 2 Corinthians 12:9).

RELEARN TRUST

Despite all possible sources of mistrust, trusting Jesus is not new for us. It is something our spirits already know how to do. It is not out of our comfort zone. It *is* our comfort zone. We all trusted Christ in the premortal world. President Lorenzo Snow taught that before the Savior "came upon earth the Father had watched His course and knew that He could depend upon Him when the salvation of worlds should be at stake; and He was not disappointed."[4] We watched Him and were not disappointed either. Consider how one young mother we'll call Karen relearned trust in God and His grace. She wrote me the following e-mail: "I have to share with you the aha moment I had a few months ago. It was Sunday, and my be-bay (baby backwards—my little nickname for my youngest daughter) rolled off the bench during sacrament meeting. She wasn't hurt. My church bag cushioned the fall. (Is that why we haul all that stuff around?) I immediately berated myself and thought, *I can't believe I let that happen. I am so lame! I am the worst mom ever.*"

Part of the reason Karen got upset at herself was because she and her family had only recently moved into the ward and were sitting by a woman Karen assumed was judging her: "We have four kids, ages six, four, two, and the be-bay. I was sure the lady thought our kids were too close together for us to be able to be good parents."

Karen had stood the baby on the bench because the people behind them were entertaining her. Then Karen got distracted by her two-year-old son, and suddenly the baby toppled. She grabbed for her, as did Sister Judgmental's husband, but neither was fast enough.

Karen wrote, "I picked up my startled baby and began comforting her; all the while I was mentally bawling myself out." When the baby quieted, Karen started wondering why she was always so critical of herself: *Why do I care so much about what that sister thinks anyway? Why, when something goes wrong, is my first response to get mad at myself? Good grief! Babies fall off benches. It happens. Get over it. Why do I get down on myself rather than just moving on?*

"Then it hit me," Karen wrote. "I realized that I don't love myself—not really. My fault-finding and saying all is lost whenever I mess up is what was modeled for me by my parents when I was growing up. Don't get me wrong. My parents are great and they are strong in the Church, but they rarely gave positive praise to my siblings and me. They rarely showed physical affection to their kids or to each other."

When Karen was in high school, she had been an outstanding athlete. However, she couldn't remember her parents ever saying, "Good job." Instead she remembered a lot of "constructive criticism" that was never constructive at all. Once when she was young she had a boyfriend even though she knew it was against Church standards. Instead of being able to talk about the situation openly with her parents, they withheld their love and gave her the silent treatment.

This young mother could finally see how all the years of disapproval had led to her perfectionistic tendencies. She said, "Nothing I do is ever good enough, and mistakes are devastating to me. As a child I felt I could never do enough to win my parents' approval, and that has carried over into my adult years. Even when my husband tells me he loves me, I usually just stare at him in disbelief and say, 'You do? Why? Are you sure?'"

Karen's aha moment was not that her parents were less than perfect. Everyone finally figures that out. The aha moment was that, almost subconsciously, she was letting the lack of trust she had in her parents translate into a lack of trust in God. Deep down, she figured that He, like her parents and the sister in her ward, was judging and criticizing. She didn't pray about mistakes or problems, because she feared receiving the same silent treatment she got from her parents.

On that turning-point Sunday, the Spirit's message was clear: "Relearn love. Relearn trust." In the weeks and months that followed, Karen focused her study time (what little a mom of four has) on the Atonement. She read several books about it and looked up scriptures about God's character and love. She also found a book about the causes of anxiety, which helped her begin to make sense of her past.

One day she read John 13:34: "A new commandment I give unto you, That ye love one another; as I have loved you." Karen said, "Those words really struck me. We are to love as *He* has loved us—not the way that parents may or may not have loved, but the way *He* has loved. I was to view myself as *He* views me."

NEWNESS OF LIFE

Professional counselor Wendy Ulrich wrote, "Often the circumstances life hands us are not the biggest problem. . . . The biggest problem is what we tell ourselves this setback or suffering means about us and about God."[5] I know a woman in Chile who had a child with Down syndrome. In her mind, this meant she must have sinned and God was punishing her. Obviously, the problem was not her little girl. It was what this woman believed her daughter's birth meant about herself and God. Imagine how this woman's life changed when two LDS missionaries told her that her daughter was not a curse from God but a blessing, and that she was a special mother to be trusted with an angel child.

This mother's experience helps us understand why Joseph Smith said, "It is the first principle of the Gospel to know for a certainty the Character of God,"[6] and if people do not comprehend the character of God, "they do not comprehend their own character."[7] The clearer the Chilean mother's view of God, the more she understood herself. Suddenly she and her daughter enjoyed a newness of life.

One of the greatest ways grace changes us is to remove our erroneous views of God and bring to our remembrance the truth we once knew so clearly. President Boyd K. Packer taught, "True doctrine, understood, changes attitudes and behavior."8

Do we believe that God is some big bully in the sky who takes delight in tormenting us and is looking for any moment when we let our guards down so He can pounce? If so, we will distance ourselves from Him. True doctrine teaches that God is a protector who has got our backs.

> *Christ's Atonement can mean development despite disaster.*

Do we see God the same way we see an envious coworker or micromanaging boss? If so, we will hide from Him. True doctrine teaches that God's "promises are sure and faithful, and that he is your friend."9

Do we see our deep, dark secrets, problems, and failures as evidence that God doesn't love us? If so, we are going to feel angry and lose faith. True doctrine assures that God understands and helps us through our problems. He knows we are learning. He knows Christ's Atonement can mean development despite disaster. Failure is an event, not a person, and, as author Patricia T. Holland once taught, "Any failure is only temporary in the gospel of Jesus Christ. The decision to carry on in spite of disappointment turns the worst circumstance into success."[10] Seeing God as our coach rather than our critic opens the door for His grace to change us.

Do we see God as aloof and apathetic? True doctrine confirms that God's hand is "outstretched" and His arm is "strong" (Jeremiah 21:5). He will reach out to us "so long as time shall last, or the earth shall stand, or there shall be one man upon the face thereof to be saved" (Moroni 7:36). Brigham Young taught, "When you . . . see our Father, you will see a being with whom you have long been acquainted, and He will receive you into His arms, and you will be ready to fall into His embrace and kiss Him."[11] That is true doctrine.

Seeing God as our coach rather than our critic opens the door for His grace to change us.

After Lehi's death, Nephi was discouraged. He had lost his father, prophet, and friend. His family was falling apart, and his brothers wanted to kill him. In that low moment, he wrote, "O wretched man that I am! Yea, my heart sorroweth because of my flesh; my soul grieveth because of mine iniquities" (2 Nephi 4:17). He was encompassed about with temptations, and even when he tried to change his attitude and rejoice, he was reminded of his sins. What saved Nephi from surrendering to

"I KNOW IN WHOM I HAVE TRUSTED"

despair and self-reproach? It was his knowledge of true doctrine. His clear view of God allowed him to trust His grace. With this trust came a new outlook on his life. He was empowered to move forward with faith. The same blessing can be ours.

When our Father in Heaven explained what was in store for us in mortality, I am sure we felt much like the daughters of Brother Robinson before they jumped in the pool. We probably felt like we were going to drown. Perhaps we screamed, cried, and kicked a little. Then, we heard Him say something like, "I've got you. I'm your father. I love you." We knew Him and trusted Him then. Through His grace we can know and trust Him again. Through every up and down in life's learning process, we can, with Nephi, declare, "I know in whom I have trusted. . . . O Lord, I have trusted in thee, and I will trust in thee forever" (2 Nephi 4:19, 34).

Chapter 7

SUCCORED BY GRACE

"Brother Wilcox, may I arrange to take the final early?" my student asked. Tyler Rostedt, the handsome young man who approached me, was in my Book of Mormon class. I knew he had served the previous summer as a young performing missionary in Nauvoo. Perhaps he needed to take the final early because of an audition or performance. I also knew Tyler was a student athlete from Australia. Did he need to go to a game? Did he simply want to take the test early so he could fly home for Christmas?

In my mind I lectured myself, *Be firm, Wilcox! You know BYU's policy! If you make an exception for one, you will have to make an exception for others!* Before I spoke aloud, Tyler continued, "You see, I was just diagnosed with a brain tumor, and the doctors need to operate as quickly as they can." The unexpected news took me completely off guard. All I could do was embrace this young man.

"Are your parents coming?" I asked.

"They don't have the money, but my ward members back home donated enough that my mom can come." Tyler then explained the miraculous way the tumor was found. He thought he had hurt a disk in his neck and went to see Dr. Brent Rich, who works with BYU athletes. Dr. Rich had Tyler get an MRI and found Tyler's neck was fine. Then he noticed a spot on the very edge of the image that didn't look quite right, so he sent Tyler for further tests. Had the MRI been a fraction of an inch lower, Dr. Rich might have missed the tumor completely.

As Tyler spoke, questions whirled in my mind: How was he holding up? How was he dealing with the fear he must be feeling? Was he angry at God? Had he received a blessing yet? Was he mature enough to see this life-altering news within a larger perspective? When my student finished speaking, I simply asked, "How are you doing spiritually?"

Tyler paused before responding, but when he finally spoke, his answer touched me deeply: "You know, Brother Wilcox, I'm okay. I really am. Just this morning in my prayers, I told Heavenly Father that if this kind of thing has to happen to people in mortality, then I am glad it happened to me and not someone who doesn't have the faith and testimony to make it through." I knew right then that no matter what happened, this boy was going to be all right.

"So, may I take the final early?" he asked. I hugged him once more and said, "Tyler, don't worry about the final. You are facing a much more important test, and I know you are going to pass with flying colors, just as you have passed my class."

What enabled Tyler to maintain faith at the very moment when so many others might lose theirs? Was he just spouting off memorized answers because of his Mormon culture? Was he just following a script? No. One look in this young man's eyes told me he truly understood the words of Alma: "And [Christ] will take upon him their infirmities, that his bowels may be filled with mercy, according to the flesh, that he may know . . . how to succor his people according to their infirmities" (Alma 7:12). This young man knew God's power and love. He knew God was teaching him, and he knew Christ would understand and strengthen him. This allowed him to make the deliberate choice to welcome grace and, with it, happiness.

POWERFUL AND LOVING

Some might say, "If there really is a God, why did Tyler get a tumor in the first place? If God is powerful, why didn't God just take it away? If God is loving, why does an innocent young man have to suffer?" These are similar to the questions one father faced when his son was diagnosed with a disease that would ultimately take his life. Years later, this father wrote a book about how he confronted the doubts and fears that surfaced when tragedy struck. His book about bad things happening to good people brought comfort to many. However, when I read it, it seemed to me that the author was saying that God is powerless to do anything about our trials except to hurt with us and love us through them, as if God just follows us from one setback to another with no plan for our lives. This view of God seemed incomplete.

In contrast, Bo Caldwell wrote *City of Tranquil Light*, a novel telling the story of her grandparents, who served as Mennonite missionaries in revolutionary China. The loss of their first child shook them both to their cores. Bo's grandmother, Katherine, addressed God as she wrote the following in her journal on April 14, 1917:

> We buried our daughter yesterday, and I am brought up short by the harshness of Your ways. I have given my all for You and in return You have taken the gift I love most—my sweet child. . . . I know You are a jealous God, but are You that jealous that You would take the other object of my devotion? I feel broken, as though there is a great gash inside of me, and my only prayer is a question: "What have You done?" I ask not from anger but from confusion, for I truly do not understand. Perhaps You are

a flawed God. . . . Perhaps it was not Your intention to take Lily, but Your inattention. Did You look away for a moment? Was Your mind elsewhere? . . . Perhaps You are at fault, not I. It seems there is so much You could have done.[1]

In her grief, Katherine poured her heart out to a God she saw as all-powerful, but not loving or attentive. I appreciate Katherine's honesty, but this part of the book left me grieving because this faithful woman's view of God seemed incomplete.

Is God impotent but caring, or is He all-powerful and aloof? How grateful I am that these are not the only options we are given. Latter-day Saints know God is powerful *and* loving. In his book *All These Things Shall Give Thee Experience*, Elder Neal A. Maxwell wrote in great detail of the afflictions through which the Prophet Joseph Smith had to pass. The Lord strengthened Joseph and taught him that his afflictions would be for his good (see D&C 122:7). God was aware of Joseph's suffering and was grieved by it. He was powerful enough to stop it, but He had a plan for Joseph. God's true love and power were demonstrated by helping Joseph through afflictions and making good come from them. God wanted Joseph to build His kingdom, but He was also determined to build Joseph in the process. Elder Maxwell wrote, "Happily, God in His omniscience can distinguish between our surface needs (over which we often pray most fervently) and our deep and eternal needs. He can distinguish what we ask for today and place it in relationship to what we need for all eternity. He will bless us, according to our everlasting good."[2]

Elder Maxwell explained that sometimes suffering comes as a consequence of our own poor choices. Other times it comes in consequence of the poor choices of others. Often it happens just because we live in a telestial world where storms blow, planes crash, children die, and wonderful young men get brain tumors. Whatever the reason for our suffering, the Lord is willing to succor and tutor us through it all. Our hardships—even those that are self-inflicted—become tools in the hands of the Master Teacher.

Sometimes bad things happen to good people "because they are the most ready to learn."[3] The closer we come to God, the more He is willing

God wanted Joseph to build His kingdom, but He was also determined to build Joseph in the process.

to teach us by requiring us to do what we don't want to do, to get what we want to get (as my friend Hal Jones used to say). "Though stretched by our challenges," wrote Elder Maxwell, "by living righteously and enduring well we can eventually become sufficiently more like Jesus in our traits and attributes, that one day we can dwell in the Father's presence forever and ever."[4]

Because God is both omnipotent and benevolent, the father who lost his son will have the opportunity to be reunited with him. Katherine will have the chance to raise her Lily. Because of the Atonement of Christ and His love and grace, these parents and children can choose to learn more about God and His plan, accept His invitation to help them grow, and be better *because* of their pain, not in spite of it. Because God is both powerful and loving, my student Tyler is not just learning a lot about cancer. He is learning a lot about Tyler.

A loving Heavenly Father can prevent our hurts, but He may not always choose to do so for the same reason a loving earthly father will not forever run behind his child's bicycle. He knows there comes a point at which protecting the child from every fall, bruise, and scrape will stifle growth. God could calm every storm, fly every airplane, heal every child, and dissolve every tumor, but "the whole program of the Father would be annulled," taught President Spencer W. Kimball. "There would be no test of strength, no development of character, no growth of powers."[5]

TEACHING AND LEARNING

Earth life was never meant to be a perpetual Garden of Eden or a twenty-four-hour amusement park. It is a school, and sometimes the best teachers are the hardest ones, and the most important courses are required rather than electives. Lessons that don't challenge us rarely change us.

"The overarching purpose of Heavenly Father's great plan

of happiness is to provide His spirit children with opportunities to learn. The Atonement of Jesus Christ and the agency [it] afforded . . . are divinely designed to facilitate our learning."[6] Jesus walked on the water, but mortality was not designed to enable us to walk on water. It was designed so that we would sink. Only then would we reach out and grasp the arm of grace extended to us. Grace is not a backup plan. It is not Plan B if we couldn't live Plan A. Grace is Plan A.

After Tyler's surgery, he felt extremely nauseous and experienced throbbing, horrific, all-night headaches. At times the pressure would feel so great that he was sure his head was going to explode. When he tried to walk he had difficulty balancing, and the left side of his body was weak and numb. Tyler's dad, Bill, and the rest of the family were keeping up with the developments long-distance. The family was worried about the pathology results that were due back soon.

It was at this time that ten teammates from BYU, all elders, gathered to give their friend a blessing, along with their coach. Tyler didn't play football or basketball, but he was at every game undercover. Although he could not disclose it at the time, Tyler was one of the young men who wore the Cosmo suit and became the energetic school mascot. After the blessing, Tyler's mom, Leanne, wrote me the following e-mail:

> I was brought to tears in the hospital room today when Tyler was surrounded by so many priesthood

holders. Before giving the blessing, Tyler's coach asked him if there was anything in particular he wanted. I was sitting there thinking that surely he would ask for the pain to be removed or to be promised a full recovery, or even that he could be made whole that very instant. Then my boy replied, "I guess I just want to know what the Lord desires me to learn from all this."

That's grace! Tyler, his mom, and their family were being strengthened by the Lord. He was giving them "grace to help in time of need" (Hebrews 4:16)—not just to be able to endure the experience but to learn from it. Those priesthood holders surrounded their teammate and anointed him with consecrated oil—a sacred reminder of Gethsemane, a lingering sign of the Atonement, and a symbolic representation of the hand of God also being placed on Tyler's head. God gives us priesthood power to enable us to bless each other. Grace is God using His priesthood power to bless us directly.

How many times have we asked, "Why this? Why now? Why me?" when the questions we should be asking are the ones asked by Tyler: "What am I to learn from this?" "How can I endure this faithfully?" Grace is not the promise of perpetual green pastures and still waters (see Psalm 23:1–2). It is the power to trust the Good Shepherd wherever He leads.

UNDERSTANDING AND STRENGTHENING

When word came back to Tyler that the tumor was cancerous, he and his family were devastated. To make matters worse, further surgery was out of the question because the tumor had merged with vital nerves that controlled his breathing, heartbeat, and blood flow. Leanne wrote, "This has been horrible to watch and experience as a mother, so I can't begin to imagine what Tyler is going through. . . . My saving grace is knowing that Christ has felt what we are feeling. My boy is not alone."

Sister Chieko Okazaki wrote, "We talk in great generalities about the sins of all humankind, about the suffering of the entire human family. But we don't experience pain in generalities. We experience it individually."[7] That is precisely why it is so vital for us to know that Jesus understands. Discussions about the strengthening power of grace can all be very academic until a young man gets a malicious brain tumor, until a mother has to watch him suffer, until a father has to deal with it from half a world away. Suddenly the needs are personal. We need to know that Jesus understands—that it is personal to Him, too.

After leaving the hospital, Tyler and his mom needed a place to stay. Dr. Rich and his wife, Lori, opened their home to them. Leanne said, "I'm still shaking my head in disbelief over those people. Who does that? Who opens their home, family, lives, everything to two strangers? Well, that's what they did for us!"

Tyler spent the next six months going through radiation and chemotherapy. Privately he wondered what was worse—the disease or the cure. He lost forty pounds and was so sick at times that he couldn't even get out of bed. He saw his athletic frame melt away and along with it all his plans, goals, and dreams for the future.

Despite the incredible help and encouragement Tyler received from others, there is only so much people can do. The ultimate help has to come from above. "Grant us, Father, grace divine" (*Hymns*, no. 170). Christ did not perform the Atonement to free us from suffering but to be able to accompany us in our suffering. What's more, He did not perform the Atonement just to be able to understand us but to assist us. He overcame in order to help us overcome. Tyler didn't need Christ to save him from death and hell at that moment. He just needed support to get through difficult days and sleepless nights. Right then, Tyler didn't need Christ to save him from his sins as much as he needed Him to strengthen him in his sorrows.

Christ did not perform the Atonement to free us from suffering but to be able to accompany us in our suffering.

I saw a bumper sticker that promised, "Whatever doesn't kill you makes you stronger." I guess it is the latest in a long line of paraphrases of the original words of German philosopher

Friedrich Nietzsche,[8] but I have to disagree with the statement, however it is phrased. It's not true. Simply going through trials does *not* make us stronger. Only Christ can make us stronger. Elder Richard G. Scott said, "Because your Father in Heaven loves you profoundly, the Atonement of Jesus Christ makes that strength possible."[9] It is His grace that empowers us to find peace when others stop seeking it. The Lord promises, "Fear thou not; for I am with thee: be not dismayed; for I am thy God: I will strengthen thee; yea, I will help thee" (Isaiah 41:10).

Grace is God's hand reaching down to us. Tyler didn't have to earn it, deserve it, or meet certain conditions to merit it. He just had to make the self-willed choice to grasp it. Tyler said, "That became harder as the months wore on. There were so many miracles associated with finding the tumor and getting through the surgery that I was on a spiritual high. Then it just turned into months and months of being sick and feeling discouraged. It's hard to feel spiritual when you are sick all the time. The physical pain is so intense that spiritually you start feeling numb." Tyler explained that he felt like a missionary making the transition home. Slowly, the spiritual highs of the mission give way to the realities of day-to-day life. "It was hard, but I knew I needed to get outside myself and draw closer to God, so I volunteered and was called and set apart to be an ordinance worker at the Provo Utah Temple. That helped me spiritually and made me happier."

Happy? I have seen people who, unlike Tyler, have survived catastrophes only to become hard-hearted and bitter. Many former prisoners of war become alcoholics and drug abusers when finally released. They escape one prison only to put themselves in another. I know former athletes who curse God because of accidents that have left them unable to perform, but Tyler was making a different choice. He was choosing grace and the happiness that comes with it.

"FLOWERS OF GRACE APPEAR"

One of the happiest hymns I know is "There Is Sunshine in My Soul Today" (*Hymns*, no. 227). We sing, "The dove of peace sings in my heart, the flowers of grace appear." Were these words written by somebody who had never experienced any trials? Not at all. The one who wrote the text of that hymn, Eliza ("Lidie") Hewitt, graduated as valedictorian of her class and started her teaching career in the late 1800s with great optimism. One day a prankster in her class hit her in the back with a slate and injured her so badly she became bedridden and was placed in a body cast for six months.

On her first day out of the cast she went outside and wrote, "There is sunshine in my soul today, more glorious and bright than glows in any earthly sky, for Jesus is my light." The flowers of grace were there, but Lidie had to look beyond the trial and choose to see them. It would have been easy for her to be resentful, to quit teaching, or to seek revenge on the child who hurt her. Instead, Lidie became the superintendent of a Sunday School at an orphanage called "The Northern Home for Friendless Children." She taught the orphans to sing "There Is Sunshine in My Soul Today" because she wanted them to know they were *not* friendless. God is powerful and loving. He was teaching them. Christ always understands and offers to help. Lidie wanted those children to know they could be happy despite difficult circumstances: "When Jesus shows his smiling face, there is sunshine in the soul."

Like Lidie, early pioneers faced challenges. Two days after arriving in the Salt Lake Valley, Brigham Young and other leaders climbed to Ensign Peak. Nauvoo and Winter Quarters were behind them. The exodus across the continent was behind them. It was time to look ahead. From the top of Ensign Peak they had a marvelous view and began to lay out plans for the city they intended to build. It was also there that they unfurled a banner (well, historians say it was really just a yellow bandanna) as an ensign to all nations (see *Hymns*, no. 5).

In 1934 a small monument was built atop the famous peak. It is not very big or impressive by today's standards, but it has great meaning for those who realize that the rocks of the monument were gathered from locations all across the Mormon Trail. The stones came from New York, Ohio, Missouri, Illinois—places where the early Saints faced rejection, hardships, and bitter persecution. That monument was made from the stones of suffering. Christ didn't suffer so we wouldn't have to. He suffered so our suffering would not be wasted. It can mean something. The monuments of our lives may never be big or impressive. They may never draw crowds, but they will stand forever as "monuments of wondrous grace" (*Hymns*, no. 164). The last time I hiked Ensign Peak was in the spring. There were little wildflowers all along the trail. I couldn't help but think of the phrase in Lidie's hymn: the flowers of grace appear. For those who choose to accept God's grace, there will always be flowers surrounding the stones. There will always be sunshine after the storms.

For those who choose to accept God's grace, there will always be flowers surrounding the stones. There will always be sunshine after the storms.

What does the future hold for my student Tyler and his family? Much remains uncertain. Leanne returned to Australia. After everything she went through with Tyler, her body was exhausted. She applied for and was granted a leave from her work. She wrote me the following e-mail:

> Brad, I already lost a baby girl early in my marriage. The prospect of burying another child has nearly been my undoing, but I am at peace. My spirit is strong even though physically I am worn out. Jesus

has carried my boy through the darkest hours. My Redeemer has sustained him in his weakest moments. My Savior has supported him through every second of pain. He has done the same for me. How can we fail to trust Him now? Sometimes He calms the storms. Sometimes He calms us in the midst of the storms. I'm good either way.

Much has happened to Tyler since he first approached me and asked if he could take his final early. Recently, Tyler said, "Who knows what's ahead? I am going to return to BYU and keep working toward graduation, but the tumor is not going away. The best the doctors can do is try to keep it from growing. I am in the Lord's hands." Tyler is choosing faith independent of outcome. He is choosing to love God without conditions. He is choosing to hope, and when it fades, he hopes for more hope. He is choosing to welcome grace and find joy, come what may.

Tyler's attitude reminds me of the words that were spoken of Alma and his missionary companions: "Yea, and [Christ] also gave them strength, that they should suffer no manner of afflictions, save it were swallowed up in the joy of Christ" (Alma 31:38). We need not fear change. In His grace the Lord has promised, "Wherefore, fear not even unto death; for in this world your joy is not full, but in me your joy is full" (D&C 101:36).

Chapter 8

SAVED BY GRACE

Once, while teaching a group of Primary children about grace, I challenged them to find the word in a hymn. The books flew open and the search was on. Within a minute, a boy raised his hand and enthusiastically declared, "It's in hymn number 249, 'Called to Serve.'"

I quickly reviewed the text in my mind and came up blank. I had sung the hymn countless times and couldn't remember the mention of grace. "Are you sure?" I asked. The boy confidently held out his book and pointed to the bottom of the page, where we all discovered the text had been written by Sister *Grace Gordon!*

One teacher quipped, "That puts a new twist on being saved by Grace!" All the adults laughed as we thought of the children picturing Grace Gordon showing up in a superhero costume.

Children are not the only ones who can misunderstand what it means to be saved by grace. Knowing a little history about the oft-repeated phrase can be helpful, along with comprehending multiple types of salvation.

BRIEF HISTORY

The Church of Jesus Christ in the meridian of time was made up of members from diverse backgrounds and cultures, just as the Church is today. There were members with Jewish heritage who emphasized strict obedience to the law and judged righteousness by outward performances. Church leaders had to remind these Saints that they were not saved by their deeds but rather by "grace through the redemption that is in Christ Jesus" (Romans 3:24; see also 3:20).

In ancient America there were also Christians who were so focused on the law that they overlooked the need for a Savior. Abinadi taught them, "Salvation doth not come by the law alone; and were it not for the atonement, which God himself shall make for the sins and iniquities of his people, that they must unavoidably perish, notwithstanding the law of Moses" (Mosiah 13:28).

Within the early New Testament Church there were other members who had come from Greek and Roman backgrounds. They had previously worshipped idols, for which there were no standard requirements. Idols don't demand much of their followers. Everyone found his or her own way. Some of these converts believed their new God—Christ—would save them no matter what they did or didn't do. To them Paul wrote, "Shall we continue in sin, that grace may abound? God forbid" (Romans 6:1–2). Or, in other words, should we just go ahead and sin because we are saved by grace anyway? No.

In ancient America there were similar believers who embraced Nehor's teachings that "all mankind should be saved at the last day" (Alma 1:4) regardless of their faith or deeds. To them Alma declared, "Repent ye, and prepare the way of the Lord, and walk in his paths, which are straight" (Alma 7:9).

Should we just go ahead and sin because we are saved by grace anyway? No.

Church leaders in both hemispheres were effectively stressing grace or works depending on the backgrounds and needs of their listeners.

After the Apostasy, the Catholic Church focused heavily on ordinances and sacraments while reformers preached scriptures and grace. This conflict set the stage for the Restoration. During the First Vision, Joseph asked which of all the churches was right, and the Savior said, "None of them." He declared, "They teach for doctrines the commandments of men, having a form of godliness, but they deny the power thereof" (Joseph Smith—History 1:19). The Lord was not pleased that His doctrines had been altered by men and that His ordinances were being performed without proper priesthood keys and authority. Through Joseph Smith, Christ's Church—complete with true doctrine and priesthood keys—was restored.

And what is the doctrine of "grace made known" (*Hymns*, no. 73)? The Book of Mormon declares, "It is only in and through the grace of God that ye are saved" (2 Nephi 10:24). In addition to scripture, consider the teachings of leaders, past and present:

• When Joseph Smith made inspired changes to the Bible, he revised Romans 3:24, which said "justified freely by his grace" to instead say "justified *only* by his grace" (emphasis in original).

• President Brigham Young taught, "When we obtain a celestial glory we shall have to explain that it is through the grace of God."[1]

• Elder Bruce R. McConkie wrote, "Does salvation come by grace, and grace alone, by grace without works? It surely does."[2]

• Elder Gene R. Cook taught, "[With] the grace of the Lord Jesus Christ, that divine enabling power to assist us, we will triumph in this life and be exalted in the life to come."[3]

• Elder Gerald N. Lund has written, "There is no need to go to extraordinary lengths to . . . explain away [Paul's] statements on salvation by grace. We *are* saved by grace."[4]

• Elder M. Russell Ballard confirmed, "No matter how hard we work, no matter how much we obey, no matter how many good things we do in this life, it would not be enough were it not for Jesus Christ and His loving grace."[5]

MANY KINDS OF SALVATION

What sets Latter-day Saints apart from other Christians is not a reluctance to acknowledge our full and complete dependence on Christ's grace but rather the possession of a full and complete understanding of salvation. Even scholars outside the Church have recognized that Latter-day Saints teach the most fully developed understanding of salvation, afterlife, and heaven of any Christian church.[6]

The word that was translated as *salvation* in many verses of the Bible could also have been rendered as *victory*. Latter-day Saints know we need victory on many battlefronts. The Book of Mormon tells of wicked Zeezrom, who ridiculed Alma and Amulek and attempted to publicly humiliate them. Later, that same Zeezrom—now repentant and sick with a burning fever—sent for Alma and Amulek to heal him (see Alma 15:5). Alma took Zeezrom's hand and asked, "Believest thou in the power of Christ unto salvation?" (Alma 15:6), or we could say, "Do you believe in Christ's power to offer victory?" Was Zeezrom thinking of being saved physically—victory over illness? Was Alma, who had been reclaimed from a life of sin, thinking of spiritual salvation or victory over sin? Either way, it is clear that "the Lord worketh in many ways to the salvation of his people" (Alma 24:27).

Elder Dallin H. Oaks has taught, "As Latter-day Saints use the words *saved* and *salvation*, there are at least six different meanings."[7] Through the Savior's grace, He offers victory over death, sin, our worst selves, ignorance, and hell. Ultimately, He offers the greatest victory of all in the form of exaltation.

DEATH

Teaching of the Resurrection, Paul wrote, "Behold, I shew you a mystery; We shall not all sleep, but we shall all be changed, . . . at the last trump: . . . we shall be changed" (1 Corinthians 15:51–52). Resurrection, victory over death, is a gift of grace. We can't do it for ourselves. The Fall of Adam and Eve brought death to mankind, and Christ came to do what no mortal could ever do—break the bands of death. However, although many Christians see the Fall as disastrous, the plan of salvation allows us to see it as desirable.

Many Christians see the Fall as disastrous, the plan of salvation allows us to see it as desirable.

In the premortal existence we had progressed as far as we could without a mortal experience, which includes receiving bodies of flesh and bones like those of our Heavenly Parents.

We honor Christ, whose unique birth made Him immortal and whose voluntary and selfless choice brought life after death. In like manner, we honor Eve, who was immortal in the Garden of Eden and whose voluntary and selfless choice brought birth after premortality.

Eve was given as a "help meet" for Adam (Genesis 2:18), but that does not mean she was his servant or partner. The term in Hebrew means more than helper. It is derived from the word *ezer*, which can also be translated as "to rescue" or "to save." Eve's righteous choice saved Adam and all of us from stagnation. Thus it is not by chance that there is a tradition of men standing when a woman enters the room.

If we knew the day Adam and Eve fell, we could rightly celebrate it just as we do Christmas and Easter. Maybe choirs of angels sang, "Glory to God in the highest" on that occasion too, for without the Fall and the opposition it brought, we could never fully appreciate the "peace" and "good will toward men" (Luke 2:14) proclaimed at Christ's birth.

Many religious leaders see our physical bodies as ugly, corrupt, and even evil. They see death as freeing our spirts from the prison of their bodies. Latter-day Saints do not see our bodies as prisons but as sacred, beautiful temples (see 1 Corinthians 6:19) and as absolutely essential to our progression. Through Resurrection, our spirits and bodies will be united eternally, "never to be divided" (Alma 11:45).

After I spoke at a treatment center for troubled teens, some of the young people approached me with questions. One girl asked, "Do you believe everyone will be resurrected?"

I responded, "Yes. I believe that is a gift Christ has given everyone."

She then shocked me by saying, "Tell Jesus to just keep His stupid gift. I don't want to be resurrected. I hate my body. It's ugly and gross. I can't wait to get rid of it." Her strong words revealed the same deep issues as her tattoos and body piercings. She had multiple scars where she had cut herself and huge gauges in both earlobes. I said, "One day, I hope you can see the beauty Christ sees in you."

"Whatever," she muttered as she turned and walked away. When we abuse or defile our sacred bodies, we disrespect a central purpose of mortality and downplay our eternal destinies. Satan and those who chose to follow him in the premortal existence forfeited the opportunity to have bodies. That's why Education Week presenter Mary Ellen Edmunds humorously calls them nobodies (no bodies!) and Scott Anderson, another favorite Education Week presenter, tells the youth, "When Satan tells you that your body is ugly, just say, 'Well, at least I have one!'" The spirits who followed Satan have such a strong desire for tabernacles of flesh that they are willing to possess swine for even a brief moment (see Mark 5:6–13). We, on the other hand, will enjoy perfected and glorified bodies forever free from every mutilation, deformity, and scar.

Often the gift of resurrection is called unconditional because everyone will be resurrected regardless of his or her choices. This is accurate at this point in time, but resurrection was conditional upon our choosing to come to earth in the first place. It seems logical that Heavenly Father could have provided immortal bodies for us. Then there would have been no need for the Resurrection. But we had much to learn, so God wisely made mortality and resurrection dependent on our choices. Those who followed Satan chose not to be resurrected when they chose not to come to earth. Our current choices here on earth and later in the spirit world will not affect whether or not we are resurrected, but they will play a part in the order in which we will be resurrected and the type of body we receive—celestial, terrestrial, or telestial (see Alma 42:27; 1 Corinthians 15:40–42; D&C 76). Author Truman G. Madsen wrote, "That we will be resurrected is an exceptionless truth. But the when of the resurrection, the how of it, and the kind of body we receive in the resurrection are conditional. They depend almost entirely on us and the relationship we forge with Him who is the resurrection and the life."[8]

Without resurrection not only would our progress be stopped, but we would regress. Joseph Smith taught that "all beings who have bodies have power over those who have not."⁹ The prophet Jacob taught that without bodies we would be subject to Satan and ultimately become like him: "O the wisdom of God, his mercy and grace! For behold, if the flesh should rise no more our spirits must become subject to that angel who fell from before the presence of the Eternal God, and became the devil, to rise no more. And our spirits must have become like unto him, and we become devils, angels to a devil, to be shut out from the presence of our God, and to remain with the father of lies, in misery, like unto himself" (2 Nephi 9:8–9).

Scriptures teach that our resurrected bodies will be incorruptible (see 1 Corinthians 15:43; 2 Nephi 9:13). That means we will not age or fall apart, but it also means Satan will not be able to corrupt us. No wonder Joseph Smith taught that happiness and joy are dependent on having a body (see D&C 93:33, 34) and that "no person can have . . . salvation except through a tabernacle."¹⁰ The Resurrection is one of many ways we are saved by grace.

SIN

Christ saved us from death, but He also offered victory over sin. His perfect life was a flawless model, but all along He knew we could not follow Him flawlessly. Paul wrote, "For all have sinned, and come short of the glory of God" (Romans 3:23). Christ came to take "away the sin of the world" (John

1:29) and offer "forgiveness of sins, according to the riches of his grace" (Ephesians 1:7). But "Christ died not to save indiscriminately but to offer repentance" taught Elder D. Todd Christofferson.[11] Because Jesus paid our debt to justice by shouldering the penalty for our sins, we can repent (see Helaman 14:18).

Picture the hopelessness of our situation if there were no second chances, no new beginnings, no clean slates, and no do overs. Imagine never being able to rid ourselves of shame and feel peace—never being able to live with God. Without Christ and the "beauties of [His] grace" (*Hymns*, no. 178), we would live in a world in which unavoidable sins could bring only regret and never reflection—a world where we would be forever tempted and never taught.

In most of the New Testament, the word *repentance* was translated from a Hebrew word meaning "to turn," as in to change course. The gift of forgiveness is correctly labeled as *conditional* because it is dependent upon our course changes. Nevertheless, the opportunity to repent and engage with Christ in a process of personal refinement is not dependent on anything. It can be labeled as *unconditional* because it is a gift.[12]

One of my students at BYU, Sarah Hill, turned in a paper she titled "The Screw-Up Letters" (a clever take on C. S. Lewis's *The Screwtape Letters*). In it she wrote, "Christ's Atonement helps me repent and be forgiven but it also enables me to learn, grow, mature, and become throughout the repentance process." She explained how Christ's gift allows her to see mistakes as stepping stones in the change process rather than just stones weighing her down. Sarah signed her paper (as we all could), "A Screw-up with Potential."

Another student wrote in her paper, "In the past I felt reluctant to repent because I saw it as embarrassing and depressing." She had seen herself starting off at one hundred percent, with each sin making her less and less. But none of us was ever perfect to start with. Repentance is not a punishment for slipping from perfection. It is a step toward that goal. The process does not take us back to one hundred percent but closer to it. She wrote, "Now each time I kneel in prayer and ask forgiveness, and each time I take the sacrament, I'm excited for the chance to start over, change, and become better. . . . I no longer see repentance as a negative thing, but as a gift of hope and love."

Repentance is not a punishment for slipping from perfection. It is a step toward that goal.

Think of a child in school who has been assigned to write a story. He is not better off by leaving his paper clean with no marks on it. A clean sheet of paper is not the goal. He needs to write his first draft. The teacher then suggests he add in more description and detail. Maybe she suggests that he use a different word here or there and fix some spelling and punctuation errors. The student returns to his desk and makes changes. A perfect first draft is not the goal, and although the child doesn't usually realize it, a polished, final draft is not the goal either. The teacher knows that improving the writing is only a way of improving the writer. Going through the writing process is how the child learns to discover what is inside him, bring it out, and share it with others. It is how he learns to think more clearly and live more observantly. Learning to write is not just a skill that will help the child make a living one day. It will help him make a life. It is the same for us as we choose to engage with Christ in the repentance process. "Sometimes we forget," wrote Elder Tad R. Callister, "that repentance is not only the road to forgiveness; it is also the road to perfection."[13]

I once asked a young man at BYU to tell me about his conversion. He said, "I don't know if you really want to hear it. I was a pretty bad kid." I assured him I did, so he told me how in elementary school he and his buddies thought it was funny to torment dogs and cats. By middle school they had turned their attention to bullying special-needs students.

"Didn't you feel bad about what you were doing?" I asked.

"Of course I did," he admitted, "but I was afraid that if I stopped or asked my friends to stop they would attack me. I guess my fear was greater than my guilt." In high school these young men would drive through town throwing water balloons at homeless people. He said, "You know those people on the roadside who hold signs asking for money? Well, we'd slow down like we were going to give them something and then we would dump buckets of cold water on them and speed off." I couldn't believe what I was hearing. The schoolteacher in me wanted to haul this kid right down to the principal's office!

The young man continued, "Then a girl at school invited me to come to a Mormon youth conference at a nearby college campus. I assumed it would be a weekend full of mischief and late-night pranks, so I agreed to go."

Instead, the teenager discovered a weekend full of workshops and evening devotionals, but he didn't complain. He actually liked it. He said, "Toward the end of the conference one of the speakers talked about how people had persecuted Christ—how the Roman guards had whipped Him, spat upon Him, and made Him carry His own cross. All at once I realized: that would have been me! It was like a dam broke inside. All the hurt I had caused, all the pain I was responsible for flooded over me, and I felt horrible."

The young man thought of the animals he had tortured, kids he had bullied, homeless people he had belittled, and he wanted to run and hide. He said, "The speaker then started talking about how the Romans crucified Jesus, and I lost it. I felt like I was swinging the hammer on the nails, and I couldn't stop crying."

One of the leaders noticed the tears, motioned for one of the other kids to move, sat next to this young man, and put an arm around his shoulder. The boy recalled, "I was embarrassed but couldn't speak. I just sobbed. I felt so bad about all the pain I had caused through the years."

Then the speaker said the words that Christ uttered from the cross, "Father, forgive them; for they know not what they do" (Luke 23:34). The boy confided, "That's when peace washed over me and I knew I would be okay. I didn't know how or why, but hearing those words made me feel like I was getting another chance." The young man had not yet encountered LDS hymns, but he discovered the truth of the text: "The very foes who slay thee have access to thy grace" (*Hymns*, no. 197). In the weeks and months that followed, this young man began attending church with his friend, met with the missionaries, and got baptized. The opportunity to repent and be forgiven is one of many ways we are saved by grace.

OUR WORST SELVES

Along with saving us from death and sin, Jesus offers us victory over our worst selves. Not only can our sins be forgiven, but we can be born again (see 2 Corinthians 5:17). Christ can become the father of our spiritual rebirths (see Mosiah 5:7). "Have ye spiritually been born of God?" asked Alma. "Have ye received his image in your countenances? Have ye experienced this mighty change in your hearts?" (Alma 5:14). The opportunity to answer yes to these questions is a gift of grace—something we cannot do on our own.

Every person born into the world is responsible for his or her own choices because, members of the Church or not, Christian or not, religious or not, we are all given the ability to distinguish between good and evil: "The Spirit giveth light to every man that cometh into the world" (D&C 84:46; see also Moroni 7:16). We call it the light of Christ (see Moroni 7:18).

Despite this gift, we make sinful choices that dull our consciences. We ignore that inborn moral compass and end up lost, confused, and unwilling to admit it was our own fault. Christ came to save us from our prideful and unrepentant selves. Through His Atonement, we can become "submissive, meek, humble, patient, full of love, willing to submit to all things" (Mosiah 3:19). "Marvel not," the Lord said to Alma, "that all mankind, yea, men and women, all nations, kindreds, tongues and people, must be born again; yea, born of God, changed from their carnal and fallen state, to a state of righteousness" (Mosiah 27:25).

Christ came to save us from our prideful and unrepentant selves.

Some associate being born again with baptism, which is an essential ordinance, but spiritual rebirth is usually a much longer process. In the perspective of the plan of salvation, being born again entails much more than the cleansing of baptism described in the Bible. It also includes the development of the soul associated with the covenants of baptism emphasized in the Book of Mormon (see Alma 7:15). As I renew baptismal covenants by taking the sacrament every week throughout my life, I engage in the process of trading my "broken heart" (3 Nephi 9:20) for "a new heart." Christ takes away my "stony heart" and replaces it with a "heart of flesh" (Ezekiel 36:26).

After we make covenants at baptism, we receive the gift of the Holy Ghost—a greater endowment of the same feelings associated with the light of Christ and the opportunity to have those feelings with us always.[14] As we follow the Spirit's promptings, He sanctifies us, smooths out our rough edges, and polishes us over time.

During World War II, Elder David B. Haight was flying in a plane over the Pacific when suddenly the engine began spewing flames and smoke. In the terror of that moment, Elder Haight poured out his heart to God. He promised that if he got out of the war alive he would rededicate his life to service in the Church. Elder Haight said, "I pondered that night that I hadn't given it my all. I didn't have my priorities in proper order. That night my whole life passed in review before me. I reappraised my life and recommitted myself to the Lord."[15]

That sincere prayer was a turning point. However, Elder

Haight was not born again the instant he made his commitment but throughout all the subsequent years that he kept it. This event was only part of strengthening a covenant relationship with the Lord that continued throughout Elder Haight's lifetime.

As an Apostle, Elder Haight visited the mission where I was serving as a young man. It was my first time seeing an Apostle in such an intimate setting. He told us that although he had a testimony of the gospel from a young age, he had not always been as active and dedicated as he should have been. "I've stolen a few apples in my time," he stated.

His heartfelt words on that occasion touched me deeply. I figured that since God could still use Elder Haight despite his less-than-perfect past, maybe He could also use me. Just as God sanctified Elder Haight, maybe He was willing to polish and refine me as well. My encounter with that Apostle so impressed me that years later I named my youngest son David after him. The chance to be born again and become our best selves is one of many ways we are saved by grace.

IGNORANCE

In Doctrine and Covenants 131:6 we read, "It is impossible for a man to be saved in ignorance." Impossible means impossible—something we can't do by ourselves. Along with saving us from death, sin, and our worst selves, Christ's grace also gives us victory over ignorance (see 2 Nephi 4:23). He does not leave us in darkness. He said, "I am the light of the world: he that followeth me shall not walk in darkness, but shall have the light of life" (John 8:12).

When young Joseph Smith felt confused, there came into his life a pillar of light. When we are unsure, we can also seek a pillar of light—a clear picture of God, our relationship to Him, and the knowledge that what we are doing is in accordance with His will and plan for us. This knowledge can save us as it saved Joseph.

I had a difficult time in middle school. A boy with no basket-shooting or football-throwing skills often suffers during early adolescence. The seventh-graders in my school came together from all over the city, so there were many new students I did not know. To make matters worse, my best friend from sixth grade moved away. I felt very alone.

Some kids attempted to mask their own insecurities by picking on others, and somehow in the shuffle I ended up at the bottom of the pecking order. Each day I faced bullying, threats, and rejection from peers. Once I was in that position, nothing I did was right. If I tried to talk and be friendly, I was mocked. If I didn't, others made fun of me for staying to myself. I hated the hurt, but—and this is the point—through it all I did not hate myself.

My parents and Church teachers had helped me connect

with the true source of all self-esteem—God. Because of that, I liked myself. Because I knew I was valuable in God's eyes, I valued myself. The fact that peers at school didn't like me did not seem to be evidence that I was a bad person. It was simply evidence that they did not yet know me.

As my classmates and I grew and matured, we came to know each other better. I reached out in service, and my efforts over time brought acceptance. In fact, when awards were passed out at my senior-class dinner dance in high school, I was not voted best looking or most likely to succeed. Instead I was given an award that meant much more to me than any other ever could. I was named the most-loved senior. This award came from some of the same students who literally spat on me in the halls of our middle school.

My self-esteem was tested, but Christ saved me from ignorance. I received a knowledge of my true self-worth. With this knowledge I was able to weather the storm.

We can feel the same sense of strength that the Prophet Joseph Smith felt during his life.

That doesn't mean that it has been smooth sailing ever since. Sadly, many adults act as though they are still in middle school. Moments of self-doubt come at every age and every stage, and we all must be reminded over and over of our eternal value. Then, in a small way, we can feel the same sense of strength that the

Prophet Joseph Smith felt during his life. Once when he was served a groundless warrant even after accusations against him had already been dismissed, he wrote, "The constable who served this second warrant upon me had no sooner arrested me than he began to abuse and insult me, and so unfeeling was he with me, that although I had been kept all the day in court without anything to eat since the morning, yet he hurried me off to Broome county, a distance of about fifteen miles, before he allowed me any kind of food whatever. He took me to a tavern, and gathered in a number of men who used every means to abuse, ridicule, and insult me. They spit upon me, pointed their fingers at me, saying, 'Prophesy, prophesy' and thus did they imitate those who crucified the Savior of mankind, not knowing what they did."[16]

These ignorant men did not know who the Prophet was. They did not esteem him. Nevertheless, Joseph knew exactly who he was. He knew his relationship to God, and he knew his worth in God's eyes. This knowledge allowed him to act accordingly and to weather storm after storm throughout his life.

Cult leaders like to keep their followers in ignorance. They encourage people to simply believe them and follow blindly. By contrast, Joseph Smith said, "God hath not revealed anything to Joseph, but what He will make known unto the Twelve, and even the least Saint . . . as fast as he is able to bear them."[17] Joseph did not want others to just believe his testimony; he encouraged them to find out the truth for themselves. He did not want others to just feel God's grace secondhand; he wanted them to receive it firsthand.

HELL

Christ offers us victory over death, sin, our worst selves, and ignorance, but also over hell. Many Christians face a dilemma. They believe God gives common grace (what we would call the light of Christ) to all people, but saving grace only to Christians. So, if everyone has to accept Jesus to be saved, what happens to those who never hear about the Savior? Years ago people taught that these souls went straight to hell, but what does that say about God's mercy? Today people teach that they will go to heaven regardless of their actions or choices. What does that say about God's justice? Only in the restored gospel do we find the answer that satisfies both mercy and justice: between death and the Resurrection all spirits will have the chance to learn of Christ and accept saving ordinances performed on their behalf. The Bible Dictionary states, "Knowledge of divine and spiritual things is absolutely essential for one's salvation; hence the gospel is to be taught to every soul" ("Knowledge," 721).

For Latter-day Saints, hell is not a pit of fire where the wicked are tormented forever. Rather, the word *hell* is used to describe a part of the Spirit world—a place of rehabilitation rather than punishment. It is a temporary state in which individuals can choose to be taught, repent, come to Christ, and progress. Ultimately, hell can also describe outer darkness, a permanent place reserved for the devil and his followers, including those who, even after receiving a body, being taught, and having every imaginable opportunity to change, deny the truth staring them in the face and choose to defect to perdition. Those who choose to join Satan in outer darkness will feel anguish—not just because they have chosen to reject repentance and suffer for their own sins but because their progress will be forever blocked and they will have no one to blame but themselves (see Helaman 14:29–31).

> We believe God is a successful parent! We believe Christ is a successful Savior!

Thankfully, these souls will not constitute the majority. I once participated in a symposium held at Brigham Young University on the topic of heaven and hell. LDS, Islamic, Catholic, and Evangelical perspectives were presented by representatives of the various faiths. A colleague and I then facilitated a question-and-answer session. One listener asked, "When all is said and done, will your heaven be larger than hell or vice versa?" Each representative responded, but it was the Mormon who described the smallest hell and the largest heaven.

We believe God is a successful parent! We believe Christ is a successful Savior! They will successfully rescue all who choose to be rescued. Because of Christ's Atonement, the vast majority of

God's children will dwell in a kingdom of glory (see 1 Corinthians 15:40–42; John 14:2). In Doctrine and Covenants 76:43 we read that Christ "glorifies the Father, and saves all the works of his hands." No wonder my daughter Wendee, when once asked how we escape hell and get to heaven, responded, "Grace-fully!" The ability to leave spirit prison and enter paradise and the opportunity to choose to be in a kingdom of glory rather than outer darkness are ways we are saved by grace.

Alma questioned the suffering Zeezrom, "Believest thou in the power of Christ unto salvation?" (Alma 15:6). We don't know what type of salvation Alma and Zeezrom were thinking about, but we know that *every* victory is because of Christ—our Savior in *every* sense of the word. Zeezrom believed, and Alma "cried unto the Lord, saying: O Lord our God, have mercy on this man, and heal him according to his faith which is in Christ. And when Alma had said these words, Zeezrom leaped upon his feet" (Alma 15:10–11).

Elder Bruce R. McConkie wrote, "There is no salvation of any kind, nature, or degree that is not bound to Christ and his atonement."[18] Through His grace we can be victorious over death and sin. We can be victorious over our worst selves and ignorance. Because of Him we can be victorious over hell and, through it all, we can be changed. Heaven will be large enough to welcome all who choose to enter—"even as many as will" (Moses 5:9).

Chapter 9

TRANSFORMED BY GRACE

Elder Dallin H. Oaks taught that we are saved in at least six ways. If you were counting, the last chapter covered only five. Salvation also means obtaining eternal life or being exalted. Many Christians see immortality and eternal life as the same thing, but Latter-day Saints understand they are different. The Lord said, "For behold, this is my work and my glory—to bring to pass the immortality and eternal life of man" (Moses 1:39). Immortality describes living forever, and eternal life describes the life lived by our Heavenly Parents. Elder Bruce C. Hafen wrote that eternal life refers not to *length* of life but to *quality* of life, which "involves the long-term, difficult, gradual development of the capacity to live like Christ."[1]

Elder Oaks has written, "This salvation requires more than repentance and baptism by appropriate priesthood authority. It also requires the making of sacred covenants, including eternal marriage, in the temples of God, and faithfulness to those covenants by enduring to the end."[2] Because of these expectations, some people assume that we are saved by grace but exalted by our own works. This is not the case. Exaltation is a gift of grace. It is grace at its finest. Grace can not only get us to heaven, but it can give us the desire to stay. This type of salvation offers victory over our first estate (premortality) and our second estate (mortal life) and constitutes the opportunity to be changed and become like God. This transformation is not possible on our own. This salvation, and the sense of mission it provides, reveals the true greatness of Christ's Atonement as it opens both the gates and windows of heaven.

BECOMING LIKE GOD

One of the most beautiful descriptions of grace is found in the scriptural term *power of godliness*. We read that it is in the ordinances of the Melchizedek Priesthood performed in holy temples that this power is manifested (see D&C 84:20). Elder D. Todd Christofferson said, "Our covenant commitment to Him permits our Heavenly Father to let His divine influence, 'the power of godliness,' flow into our lives."[3] This includes both the power to deny ourselves of all ungodliness (see Mormon 10:32) and the power to become "partakers of the divine nature" (2 Peter 1:4).

In Doctrine and Covenants 84:23–24 we read that Moses wanted to prepare his people to see the "face of God," but "they hardened their hearts and could not endure his presence." The power of godliness was needed so they could "see the face of God, even the Father, and live" (D&C 84:22). But seeing the face of God was not the ultimate goal for Moses' people any more than it is the goal for us today. Everyone will see the Lord at the judgment. The power of godliness will not only allow us to see His face and live but also to live so that the Lord can see His countenance in us (see Alma 5:14). It is the power to live as He lives, love as He loves, create as He creates, and experience the joy He experiences.

Latter-day Saints have taken a lot of criticism over the years for teaching that humans have godly potential. Writers of movies and Broadway musicals have all taken their turns ridiculing this doctrine, but their disapproval doesn't change the fact that this type of salvation is real. In fact, it is in this salvation that we find the full meaning of all other types of salvation.

What is the purpose of resurrection and forgiveness if they only restore the status quo? To what end are we born again if we cannot also be reared to spiritual adulthood? What is the purpose of escaping ignorance

The power of godliness will not only allow us to see His face and live but also to live so that the Lord can see His countenance in us.

and hell if heaven does not offer something more than becoming harp-strumming angels sitting on clouds? What good is life after death if progress ends? What good is finally reaching heaven if we cannot use what we have learned to help and benefit others? The answers to all these questions are found only in discovering and embracing our celestial potential.

Upon listening to the devotional address I gave at Brigham Young University on the topic of grace, one evangelical leader wrote me the following e-mail: "It made me glad to see that the Mormons are finally beginning to accept the evangelical doctrine of grace and give up Joseph Smith's foolish teachings concerning God's nature and man's capacity to somehow be like Him."

I responded, "I am honored that you took time to listen to my talk, but the understanding I shared of grace is not borrowed from or modeled after evangelical teachings. Rather, it is based solidly on Joseph Smith's revelations. We believe man's capacity to become like God is right at the center of the doctrine of grace because grace is the power to be changed."

In the *Lectures on Faith* we read, "All those who keep his commandments shall grow up from grace to grace, and become heirs of the heavenly kingdom, and joint heirs with Jesus Christ; possessing the same mind, being transformed into the same image."[4]

Many religious people refer to God as our Heavenly Father,

but they see this as a figurative and metaphorical relationship. Not so for us. In the context of the plan of salvation we know that God is not "kind of like" our father and we are not "kind of like" brothers and sisters. We believe we are literally begotten and beloved spirit "children of the most High" (Psalm 82:6), the "offspring of God" (Acts 17:29). There are several Hebrew words for God, but all express "one very important Israelite concept: divine kinship, or kinship with God."[5] Andrew C. Skinner, former dean of religious education at BYU, wrote, "God and men are the same divine, eternal species, and if we do not comprehend the nature of God, we cannot appreciate our divine parentage nor the very real potential we possess to become like our heavenly parents."[6]

SENSE OF MISSION

This knowledge emboldens us at the same time that it humbles us. It makes us feel secure, and at the same time we feel small. It is at once a blessing and a huge responsibility. Consider how these paradoxes combine to motivate us and provide a sense of mission. What kept Christopher Columbus going when others gave up? How did he endure years of ridicule and forge ahead through every disappointment, mutiny, and shipwreck? Clark B. Hinckley wrote, "Columbus had an unshakable sense of mission."[7]

Think of the sense of mission felt by Saul. He went from

persecuting the early Saints to being persecuted at their sides. What kept him going through years of rejection and imprisonment? Saul discovered he was a "chosen vessel" (Acts 9:15). That knowledge sank deep into his soul, motivating great self-discipline and willingness to sacrifice. It provided the sense of mission that changed his name, his life, and ultimately the world.

A sense of mission allows all of us to feel more intense joy and more profound love than what is felt by those who do not share this knowledge.

When we as Latter-day Saints catch even a glimpse of who we really are and all that awaits us, it provides the same unshakable sense of mission felt by Columbus, Paul, and many others. Think of how a sense of mission changed Esther, Abish, and Moses. It transformed how they saw and treated themselves and all those around them. Think of how a sense of mission altered Ammon, Moroni, Abinadi. It changed how they measured success and failure. A sense of mission allows all of us to feel more intense joy and more profound love than what is felt by those who do not share this knowledge. We can appreciate the beauty of the world and order of the universe with heightened awareness. We can step away from the routines of sleeping and waking up to seek and find greater purpose in mortality than mere existence. We, like the Saints and poets described in Thornton Wilder's

Our Town, can truly "realize life while [we] live it—every, every minute."[8]

When Adam and Eve partook of "the tree of the knowledge of good and evil" (Genesis 2:17), God declared they had "become as one of us" (Genesis 3:22). This announcement underscores the central purpose of the plan of salvation and helps us recognize the seeds of godhood within each of us. In Romans 12:2 we read, "Be not conformed to this world: but be ye transformed." Many similar Bible verses hint at our eternal potential, but Latter-day Saints do not teach this doctrine based on the Bible alone.

There is evidence that early Christians were much more aware of this sacred doctrine than modern Christians,[9] but that is not why we believe. Great writers throughout history, including William Shakespeare[10] and Robert Browning,[11] have alluded to this truth, but that is not the foundation of our faith. We believe because of revelations given to Joseph Smith (see D&C 76:53, 58; 88:107) and because of the teachings and testimonies of all his successors.

When Christian friends have told me it is blasphemous to believe we can become like God and Christ, I have sometimes responded using the same questions Elder Tad R. Callister once asked: "Do not all Christian Churches advocate Christlike behavior? Is that not what the Sermon on the Mount is all about? If it is blasphemous to think we can become as God, then at what point is it not blasphemous to become like God—90 percent, 50 percent, 1 percent? Is it more Christian to seek partial godhood than total godhood?"[12]

GREATNESS OF THE ATONEMENT

For many Christians the greatness of Christ's Atonement is demonstrated by emphasizing human sin and the immense distance that exists between us and God. For Latter-day Saints the greatness of Christ's Atonement is illustrated by emphasizing human potential and the incredible closeness that can exist between us and God. Christ's greatest salvation is seen in His willingness to interact with us as we develop His celestial attributes.

I have often asked my students at BYU to write a paper about what the Atonement means to them. One, Kayci Nielsen, showed great understanding when she wrote, "Since we are completely dependent on the Atonement and saved by grace, does that mean that it doesn't matter what we do in this life? No! God expects us to use His grace to live righteously because those choices determine who we become."

It is this development I emphasized to the young woman who wrote me the following e-mail: "Why not have sex with my boyfriend? We can always repent later."

My response: "You can repent! You can be completely forgiven! But cleanliness is only one of God's many attributes.

There are others that must also be developed to become more like Him. The time spent breaking this commandment could be better spent developing the selflessness, self-control, patience, charity, and courage that living the law of chastity fosters."

Setting aside the fact that the choices this young couple are making carry with them physical and emotional consequences, by knowingly choosing to sin and preplanning repentance, they are taking God's mercy and forgiveness for granted. This coldness, more than anything, demonstrates that they have not yet felt a change of heart. No doubt they will be welcomed by the Savior whenever they decide to come to Him, but they will regret the time they lost.

Joseph Smith declared, "If you wish to go where God is, you must be like God, or possess the principles which God possesses. . . . Search your hearts, and see if you are like God. I have searched mine, and feel to repent."[13] Perhaps "the news of gospel grace" (Hymns, no. 321) is not just that we can be made clean and qualify to enter the presence of God but that we can be made holy enough to feel comfortable there; not just that He can love us but that He can come to trust us.

One returned missionary wrote, "My trainer was great and we followed mission rules with exactness. My next companion was the polar opposite—sleeping in until noon, never studying, and goofing off for most of the day. I quickly became a disobedient missionary. . . . I was discouraged a lot and was being chastised by the Spirit, but I pushed it away and used my discouragement as an excuse for sleeping in and not working. The thing that finally got me was my feelings when I was with my mission president. I felt so uncomfortable that I wanted to hide under a rock. I knew I would feel the same way in front of my Savior if I didn't ask God to help me change. I'm happy to report that I finished my mission strong. The final interview with my mission president was very comfortable. I had regained his trust."

How will we feel when we meet the Savior? The answer depends on how like Him we have become. On that day I will not be able to shrug my shoulders and lamely declare, "I'm only human"—not when He has offered to make me so much more than that.

How will we feel when we meet the Savior? The answer depends on how like Him we have become.

I once heard an evangelical leader respond to the following question: "Will family relationships continue beyond the grave?" He said, "Family relationships are a temporary provision. The only relationship that will matter eternally is the one we have with Jesus." To emphasize this point he said, "My wonderful mother died recently of cancer. I loved her very much. However, if when I die she attempts to stand between the Lord and me, I will push her out of the way and run to Him."

I realize he was not speaking for all evangelicals, and he was only giving a hypothetical example, but I couldn't help feeling saddened by his words. I am convinced that if what this man described were to ever really happen, the first words out of the Savior's mouth would be, "You have much yet to learn. Please go greet your mother and thank her for all she has done for you."

Receiving what God has could happen in an instant. Developing His traits takes longer—much longer. Elder Bruce C. Hafen and his wife Marie wrote, "Without our complete engagement, the problem is not that the Lord's grace *won't* help us grow, but that it *can't*. . . . Were it otherwise, in our pre-earth life our Father could have simply given us enough grace and strength to perfect us instantly."[14] This would have made obtaining a body and life on earth completely unnecessary. God would never have put us through mortality if He could have accomplished the same purpose by giving us an immortal body instantly and spiritual maturity with a wave of His hand.

PRACTICING AT-ONE-MENT

Scriptures speak of being changed in the "twinkling of an eye," but that phrase describes how *some* people will be resurrected (see D&C 43:32; 63:51; 101:31; 3 Nephi 28:8). It does not describe the transformation of our spirits.

Consider this message I received from a frustrated elder in the MTC: "Where is God? Why has He abandoned me? I have been here three weeks and I still don't speak Spanish!"

I replied to his e-mail and in the subject line I wrote, "Reality check!" I reminded him how long it takes babies to learn a language and encouraged him to be patient as he goes through similar developmental phases.

He wrote back, "But don't we believe in the gift of tongues?"

I responded, "We certainly do, and there are moments recorded in Church history when that gift was instantaneous. However, usually God's miracles take more time. It does not mean He is less involved or His grace is less present. It simply means some miracles are performed for a different purpose." Miracles are defined as interventions by God in human events. Nothing is said about the length of those interventions.

God doesn't just want this elder to look like he knows Spanish or to memorize enough to skim by for a day or two. He wants him to teach and bear a powerful testimony in Spanish. He wants him to be able to understand people's deepest concerns and fears and be able to answer their most heartfelt questions in Spanish. In addition, He wants him to be able to relate to and empathize with others as they learn. The language—and the process of learning it—need to become part of him.

God wants all of us to internalize the gospel in the same

way. We must become fluent in it. It can't be faked temporarily or put on when people are watching. It can't be reserved only for Sunday. It has to sink deep within us and become part of who we are "at all times and in all things, and in all places" (Mosiah 18:9).

Have you ever seen someone greet a stranger in a foreign language and then look lost when the stranger believes the person really can speak that language and tries to carry on the conversation? Have you ever seen people smile for a camera and stop smiling the minute the picture has been taken? Living the gospel is more than appearances, and it is the struggle of learning to live the gospel that internalizes it.

Living the gospel is more than appearances, and it is the struggle of learning to live the gospel that internalizes it.

Contrary to popular belief, it is not all about the resume. It is about what's beneath it. I know a man who, though not LDS himself, loves to hire Mormons because he is so impressed with their honesty, family focus, and work ethic. Once he received a resume from a young man who listed his mission and BYU degree, and the man hired him on the spot. Later he told me, "That was a big mistake. I've never been so disappointed. On his resume he looked like the other Mormons I have hired. Later, I found out he has left the Church and has severe problems with alcohol and drugs that are affecting his work and my business. I call him the empty suit, because he looked the part but didn't live it."

Karl G. Maeser, the spiritual architect of the very university listed on this young man's resume, said, "Knowledge is not power unless it is sustained by . . . character."[15]

Most of us have crammed for a test at school. We quickly memorized the answers and somehow passed the test. That same process won't work when it comes to passing life's tests. We can't memorize the right answers and forget them the very next day. We can't cheat by writing them on the bottoms of our shoes. They must be written on our hearts.

Compare cramming for a test to learning the Pledge of Allegiance. Most Americans know it well because we practiced it almost every day for many years. Even when my mom was struggling with dementia, she could recite the pledge. It had become part of her. God's grace is not offered to help us cram for the final judgment but to help us practice at-one-ment—becoming one with God. I don't recall the exact day when I went from not knowing the Pledge of Allegiance to having it memorized. I don't remember the exact day when I switched from not knowing Spanish to speaking it fluently. They were both internalized over time, but now they are part of who I am. In the same way, time is the medium through which the power of the Atonement is made manifest in our lives.

Some might ask, "So if becoming like God is just a matter of developing traits and practicing skills, then isn't such talk just another way of saying we are saved by our works rather than by Christ?" Absolutely not. Transformation is something we could never do for ourselves no matter how long we practice on our own. It is the divine help, feedback, direction, and mentoring we receive along the way that makes ultimate perfection possible. Coming to Christ is not the end but the means to the real end of becoming more like Him.

The Atonement is not just a favor Christ did for us—suffering so we wouldn't have to. If that were the extent of it, then we could have paid justice ourselves (see D&C 19:16–17). Christ's Atonement is much more than that. It is an investment He made in us. The favor He did for us met the demands of justice and opened the gates of heaven so we could return to the Lord's presence to be judged. The investment He made in us opened the windows of heaven through which He can cleanse us, remove our guilt, tutor us, perfect us, and exalt us—help He alone can give and without which we would be forever limited.

HEAVEN'S GATES AND WINDOWS

President Dieter F. Uchtdorf has taught about grace unlocking both the gates and windows of heaven.[16] I see open gates meaning we can have clean hands. Open windows mean we can have pure hearts. Open gates mean we can be justified. Open windows mean we can be sanctified. Open gates mean we can be ready and able to enter. Open windows mean we can be willing and desirous. *Thrones, kingdoms, principalities, glory,* and *eternal lives* (see Romans 2:7; D&C 75:5; 128:12, 23; 132:19, 24) describe what await us through open gates, but also correspond to what Christ can help us become through open windows.

God is not just preparing mansions for us. He is preparing us for the mansions. My daughter Wendee occasionally enjoys watching shows about how contractors and companies pull together to provide a dream home to someone in need. Then she read an article reporting how many of these recipients end up losing the homes within the first year because they do not have the income or skills to maintain the homes. In many cases, the dream homes become nightmares because the occupants are unprepared. This is the reason God worries about the construction of celestial souls as well as celestial mansions. Our construction is different because, unlike bricks and boards, we are free to act and are not simply to be acted upon (see 2 Nephi 2:14, 26). "God will not act to make us something we do not choose by our actions to become. . . . Through the Atonement of Jesus Christ and His grace . . . we are enabled to develop a Christlike character. Justice demands, however, that none of this happen without our willing agreement and participation."[17]

Jesus has said, "Learn of me" (Matthew 11:29), "Follow me" (John 12:26), "Keep my commandments" (John 15:10), "Walk with me" (Moses 6:34). By so doing we are not trusting in works more than grace. We are simply allowing Christ to prepare us as no one else can. Practice doesn't make perfect. Christ makes perfect (see D&C 76:51–53, 69). Without Christ's tutoring, we would be helpless. Without our willingness, His help would be halted. The Bible Dictionary states that "grace cannot suffice without total effort on the part of the recipient" (697). This "total effort" is not how we prove ourselves worthy of His offering. It is how we honor and take advantage of it. It's how we use it to His glory.

We are not racking up points to win a contest or earning some big trophy in the sky. Such views trivialize the complexities and difficulties of our mortal experiences. In the Sermon on the Mount, Jesus promised, "Great is your reward in heaven" (Matthew 5:12). It appears that reaching heaven is not the only goal. Something more awaits us *in* heaven. Jesus was teaching of exaltation. With this understanding, salvation becomes more than questioning, "How much can I get away with and still make it to heaven? What is the minimum cutoff? What is the least I can do?" Salvation becomes desiring to be perfected and humbly asking, "What lack I yet?" (Matthew 19:20).

Practice doesn't make perfect. Christ makes perfect.

Repentance is not getting away with something, but rather finally getting started on something.

Romans 5:11 is the only New Testament verse that uses the word *Atonement*. In place of it, Bible translators often used the word *reconciliation* (see Romans 5:10; 11:15; 2 Corinthians 5:18–20; Ephesians 2:16; Colossians 1:20). The word describes the mending of a broken relationship, closeness where once there was distance. Elder Bruce R. McConkie defined reconciliation as "the process of ransoming man from his state of sin and spiritual darkness and of restoring him to a state of harmony and unity with Deity."[18] Such harmony and unity is not just the result of man and God finally getting back together. True reconciliation means we will have become similar.

Often, Christmas gives us many opportunities to reflect on "the dawn of redeeming grace" (*Hymns*, no. 204). I have a friend who is serving a prison sentence. He once sent a Christmas card in which he wrote, "Lots of men here get pretty depressed in December. It is a strange phenomenon since this time of year is really no different from any other. Why is Christmas harder? I think it is because it reminds them of the ideal—the perfect family, the perfect tree and decorations. They think of the perfect meal and perfect gifts and realize how far their lives are from that ideal. The 'happiest time of the year' becomes the saddest for them." Such is the danger of celebrating Christmas without Christ. It becomes a reminder of how imperfect we are instead of a celebration of the one who came to change all that.

At Christmas we read of the wise men who came to King Herod asking where they might find the Christ child. King Herod sent the wise men to Bethlehem, saying, "When ye have found him, bring me word again, that I may come and worship him also" (Matthew 2:8). Of course, once the wise men found Jesus they were "warned of God in a dream that they should not return to Herod," whose motives were wicked. Instead, after encountering the Christ, "they departed into their own country *another way*" (Matthew 2:12; emphasis added).

When we encounter Christ, we are meant to be changed. We are meant to return to heaven another way.

When my son-in-law Landon was serving his mission in Uruguay he got to call home on Christmas and his father, Larry Laycock, a wise man himself, reminded Landon of this story. He said, "Once the kings found Christ they went home by another route, but it could also mean that they themselves were different." When we encounter Christ, we are meant to be changed. We are meant to return to heaven another way.

Christ's mission is to bring to pass our immortality and eternal life (see Moses 1:39). To that end, Jesus Christ is not a figurine in a Christmas manger scene. He is not a statue or a painting. He is real. His birth and life are not a folktale or fable. They are real. His Atonement is not a myth. It is real, and the power—the grace—that His Atonement makes possible is not a lucky charm. It is not wishful thinking or self-fulfilling prophecy. It is real. I have seen grace change others. I see it changing me.

Chapter 10

MUCHAS GRACIAS

In Spanish the word for thank you is *gracias*, which is almost identical to *gracia*, the word for grace. My friend Omar Canals, an amazing translator, told me that both words share the same Latin root, *gratia*. "From a linguistic point of view there may not be much of an association in terms of meaning," he said. "However I see a principle being portrayed by the connection: Grace should elicit gratitude." We should receive the gift of grace the same way we receive any gift—with a thank you.

In English the words *gratitude* and *grace* may not share as close of a relationship as they do in Spanish, but the same principle applies. Our works are not efforts to save ourselves. Rather, they flow from our changed and thankful hearts. They become our "grateful songs for [His] love and grace" (*Hymns*, no. 91).

MUCHAS GRACIAS

My friend Brett Sanders once told me, "Gratitude has always been the fundamental touchstone of my spirituality. When I feel truly grateful, I know the Spirit is with me and I am on the path. When I struggle to feel grateful, I know I have strayed."

Elder Dale G. Renlund confirmed, "The closer we are to Jesus Christ in the thoughts and intents of our hearts, the more we appreciate His innocent suffering, the more grateful we are for grace."[1]

Many years ago I had the opportunity to travel to Guatemala to supervise student teachers who were participating in a BYU study abroad program. My oldest son, Russell, a young teenager at the time, was with me. On the final night of our trip I was invited to speak to a local group of youth and young single adults. Afterward, I directed some games using a large, six-foot inflatable ball. Half the group stood in a circle and tried to keep the ball inside while the other half lay down on the floor and tried to kick it out. One young man kicked the ball with enthusiasm. I tried to block it with the same enthusiasm, but I instantly knew I had made a big mistake, because I felt something tear in my shoulder.

I concealed the pain the best I could and made it through the rest of the evening, but later that night I knew I had done some serious damage. While Russell slept I sat up most of the night cradling my arm as the pain became more and more intense. In the morning we went to the airport. Russell knew I was really hurting so he carried our luggage by himself. We re-entered the United States in Dallas, and by the time we made it through customs Russell could tell I had reached the end of my rope. He said, "Dad, how can I help?"

I said, "Russell, go ahead to our gate where we are going to catch the flight to Salt Lake. Look for a man wearing garments and ask if he will please come give me a blessing." Obediently, Russell ran ahead, spotted a garment line beneath a man's shirt, and told him the situation. The man came immediately. We found a private corner and he blessed me that the pain would ease until I got home and could seek medical help.

The flight to Utah was no cake walk, but, thanks to the blessing, I made it. Debi was waiting for us in Salt Lake and rushed me to the hospital. In all the hurry I didn't get the name of the man who blessed me. I have never been able to contact him to thank him. All I can do is remember him and try to do for others what he did for me.

He gave me a great gift. I didn't merit it, but I needed it. I didn't earn it, but I asked for it. That man did something for me I couldn't do for myself. Similarly, we receive God's gift of grace though we don't merit or earn it. We just need it—desperately! As we ask for His help, God can do for us—and with us—what we cannot do for ourselves. He doesn't ask for us to repay Him. All He asks is that we remember Him and strive to offer grace to others as generously as He has offered it to us. That is how we can say, "Thank you."

REMEMBER

As we partake of the sacrament, we promise to remember Christ always (see D&C 20:77). Elder Dale G. Renlund taught, "To draw closer to the Savior, we must increase our faith in Him, make and keep covenants, and have the Holy Ghost with us. . . . All of these elements come together in the sacrament. Indeed, the best way I know of to draw closer to God is to prepare conscientiously and partake worthily of the sacrament each week."[2]

My sister-in-law Cheryl Harward Wilcox came to value the sacrament much more as she helped care for her mother, Melva, until she passed away at age ninety-two. Melva was in the hospital in Payson, Utah, when it was decided that there was nothing more that could be done except to keep her as comfortable as possible until she passed on. As preparations were being made to transport her back to her home, two brethren from a local ward came into the room and asked Cheryl if her mother would like the sacrament. At first, Cheryl told them,

> *We receive God's gift of grace though we don't merit or earn it. We just need it—desperately! As we ask for His help, God can do for us—and with us—what we cannot do for ourselves.*

"No, thank you." Her mom could hardly swallow. Then Cheryl said, "On second thought, let me ask her." Cheryl leaned close to her mother's ear and said, "There are two priesthood holders here. Would you like to try to take the sacrament?"

In a faint but clear voice, Melva answered, "Yes."

Cheryl picked up a piece of bread from the tray, broke off the tiniest crumb, and gently placed it in her mother's mouth. Melva worked on it for a bit, and Cheryl quietly apologized to the men that it was taking a while. They assured her it was okay. Next Cheryl took a small plastic cup of water and held it to her mother's lips. Melva took only a small sip, and Cheryl was surprised at how well she swallowed it. Cheryl thanked the brethren, and they left for the next room. Melva died peacefully about an hour later.

In the days that followed, Cheryl realized what a sacred moment she had been allowed to share with her mother. It was her last supper. The final thing Melva did in this life was to partake of the sacrament. The final word she spoke was, "Yes." She said yes to receiving the sacrament, yes to offering her sacrifice of "a broken heart and a contrite spirit" (3 Nephi 9:20), yes to taking upon herself the name of Jesus Christ and promising to always remember Him, yes to receiving His spirit. The last things that passed through her lips were the sacrament bread and water.

As Cheryl later reflected on this special moment, she said, "How sweet her last supper must have tasted to her. Although too weak to move or speak, how alive in Christ her spirit must have felt! How grateful she must have been for His enabling power that carried her through those final moments of her mortal journey and for His promise of exaltation ahead."

Each week as we partake of the sacrament, let us be a little more mindful of what we are doing. Let us do it "in remembrance of his grace" (*Hymns*, no. 176). Then the bread and water can be "sweet above all that is sweet" for us (Alma 32:42), just as it must have been for Melva.³

Each week as we partake of the sacrament, let us be a little more mindful of what we are doing.

GRACE FOR GRACE

In scriptures we read the phrase *grace for grace* (see D&C 93:12), which describes our goal of giving grace to others as it is given to us. As grace changes us we will begin to feel it flow from us as naturally as it flows from Christ. The phrase is related to another scriptural phrase: *saviors on Mount Zion* (see Obadiah 1:21). Sometimes those who are not Latter-day Saints are bothered when we speak of being saviors. We are certainly not claiming to take the place of our Savior, but rather to stand with Him and offer grace—directly or vicariously—to others just as He does. Surely this is what Paul was communicating when he began so many of his epistles saying, "Grace be unto you" (Philippians 1:2; Colossians 1:2; 1 Thessalonians 1:1).

In *Les Misérables,* by Victor Hugo, we felt sorry for the ex-convict Valjean as he was turned away from every inn and residence. Finally a kind bishop took him in. Despite the bishop's generosity, that night Valjean stole his silver table settings and ran away. The police caught Valjean and doubted his claim that the silver had been a gift. They dragged him back to the bishop's home, where Valjean was amazed to hear the bishop corroborate his story and offer him the candlesticks he had "forgotten." The bishop's act of grace filled Valjean with such gratitude that he spent the rest of his life giving charitable gifts to others. He returned grace for grace.

Is such a change the stuff of novels and musicals and nothing more? No. The reason we love Valjean's story is because it represents with accuracy the true experiences that happen all around us—the stories we can be part of.

A few years ago I was asked to speak at a conference in Park City, Utah. One of the other presenters was Dan Gifford, founder of Cause for Hope, an organization that is helping people in developing countries to become self-reliant. The foundation's purpose is to create self-reliance through mentoring. It provides training and loans, but most important, it helps people change habits by providing mentors for them. The results have been remarkable.

Wilber, a father of four in his forties, was working as a laborer earning about a hundred dollars a month, only enough to feed his family once a day. It was a stressful time in his life. Then a new job opportunity was offered to Wilber, but he had to have a vehicle in order to travel from one facility to another, and Wilber had no transportation. He sought a loan from the foundation to buy a motorcycle and received self-reliance training. The day his loan was granted, he returned to his home and announced to the family that he would now be able to accept the new job and earn more money. His youngest son came forward, tugged on his pant leg, and asked, "Papa, does this mean we can now eat more than once a day?" Tears of gratitude filled Wilber's eyes as he answered, "Yes, son, now we can eat three times a day." Wilber's mentor taught Wilber and his family how to budget, save money, and set goals. Within a year Wilber paid off his loan, and he has now developed a savings account for his children's educations and missions. Wilber is now serving as a bishop.

Manuel was an upholsterer working in a large city. He and his wife had six sons, all under the age of eighteen. With the threat of gang violence surrounding them, they worried for the safety of their boys and decided to move to a smaller town. That meant that Manuel no longer had a job. LDS missionaries began teaching the family, and they were baptized four months later. With the help of the Cause for Hope Foundation Manuel started a small upholstering business in his new home. A mentor taught him how to keep track of income and expenses and how to advertise and acquire new clients. His business prospered, and now he has purchased some equipment that will allow him to complete jobs more quickly. He has expanded from home furnishings to car interiors. His increased income has allowed him to provide better for his family and also to serve in the Church. He is currently serving as the stake financial clerk.

Maria supported her family by making and selling tortillas out of her home. Despite her hard work, she and her children lived in poverty. She approached the foundation seeking a loan so she could improve her home-based business. The money was important and allowed her to buy supplies and some large griddles to place over the fire so she could produce more than one tortilla at a time. More important, her mentor helped her understand how to manage her income—how to figure out what was profit and what needed to go back into the business. The mentor showed her how to pay tithing, put some money in savings, and then budget the rest of the funds so her family could survive. Not only have they survived, but they have thrived. She has been able to hire some extended family members to help her growing business. She has paid off her debts and her small home. She said, "I get up early and work hard every day because I never want to go back to where I was before. Low income and high levels of debt left me feeling stressed all the time. Now I am self-sufficient. The habits my mentor has taught me have changed my life."

The reason Dan's stories touched me so deeply when I heard them is that they are not just the typical stories of people giving and receiving charity. They are stories of people giving and receiving grace for grace. People who have received help and mentoring are now turning to help and mentor others. I am thrilled for the changes that are happening in the lives of Wilber, Manuel, Maria, and their families, but in my mind these stories are not just about them. They are about the unnamed mentors who have stood by them and encouraged them throughout the process. None of these "success stories" happened overnight. They happened over years, and mentors have been there, as Christ is, the entire time.

Dan said, "I have received grace from God in such abundance. How can I not turn and try to serve, bless, and uplift others in the same way?" I wholeheartedly support what Dan and his colleagues are attempting to do. They are striving to build Zion, where we can be "of one heart and one mind" and dwell in righteousness with no poor among us (Moses 7:18). Building Zion is a cause in which I hope we can all become engaged.

Now Wilber will teach his ward members the value of self-reliance. Manuel will help his sons go on missions instead of seeing them join gangs. Maria will bless members of her extended family with employment. They will give thanks to those who have helped them by helping others. They will offer grace for grace.

Elder David B. Haight expressed the same intent when he said, "There are so many hands to shake, so many smiles to smile, so many eyes to look into, and so many hearts to touch, that I ask, 'How can I go faster and more effectively serve in the kingdom?'"[4]

One of my favorite stories in scripture is about the lame man who is carried to Christ by his friends. I love how those determined souls were not dissuaded by the crowds. They climbed to the roof and broke it open so they could lower their needy friend to the Savior (see Mark 2:1–12). Often in life I have felt like the disabled man in desperate need of help and healing, carried to Christ by wonderful friends and family members who have never given up on me. Other times I have tried to be the one who carries those around me. I'm not keeping score. I'm just keeping at it.

"Because I have been given much, I too must give" (*Hymns*, no. 219). Just as I have been forgiven, I "plead for grace . . . that [I] might forgive another" (*Hymns*, no. 140). As I have received hope and comfort, I must "give hope and comfort to the poor in memory of [His] grace" (*Hymns*, no. 310). Just as I have seen Christ's grace "foil the tempter's power" (*Hymns*, no. 166), I must help others resist temptations. Just as I have been changed through His grace, I must help others in the journey.

Then together we can sing, "Thy works of grace, how bright they shine!" (*Hymns*, no. 147). For whether we are carried or carrying, we all draw closer to Christ.

I love Spanish. There are words in that language that mean more and are more beautiful to me than any equivalents in English. Ever since my first mission to Chile many years ago, I have always silently renewed my baptismal covenants each week in Spanish. One of the words I say during those personal moments is *gracias*. To me it communicates more than thanks. It speaks also of grace. Each Sunday I think of my Savior and my covenant relationship with Him. I promise to remember Him and offer grace to others as He offers it to me. I reflect on my life and ask that I can continue to be changed through His grace. With great gratitude I close my eyes and pray, "Much thanks for Thy much grace—*muchas gracias por tu mucha gracia.*"

Whether we are carried or carrying, we all draw closer to Christ.

NOTES

ACKNOWLEDGMENTS

1. *Teachings of Presidents of the Church: Joseph Smith* (Salt Lake City: The Church of Jesus Christ of Latter-day Saints, 2007), 352.

INTRODUCTION

1. Camille Fronk Olson, "Saved and Enabled by the Grace of Jesus Christ" in *Shedding Light on the New Testament: Acts–Revelation*, ed. Ray L. Huntington, Frank F. Judd, and David M. Whitchurch (Provo, Utah: Religious Studies Center, Brigham Young University, 2009), 49.

CHAPTER 1

1. Dieter F. Uchtdorf, "The Gift of Grace," *Ensign*, May 2015, 107.
2. D. Todd Christofferson, "Free Forever, to Act for Themselves," *Ensign*, November 2014, 19.
3. *True to the Faith: A Gospel Reference* (Salt Lake City: The Church of Jesus Christ of Latter-day Saints, 2004), 78.

NOTES

4. Sheri Dew, *Amazed by Grace* (Salt Lake City: Deseret Book, 2015), 4.
5. Gérald Caussé, "For When I Am Weak, Then Am I Strong," BYU Devotional Address, 3 December 2013, 6.
6. Dietrich Bonhoeffer, *The Cost of Discipleship* (New York: Touchstone, 1995), 43–45.
7. John MacArthur, *The Gospel According to Jesus* (Grand Rapids, Michigan: Zondervan, 1988), 15–16.
8. See David Kinnaman and Gabe Lyons, *UnChristian: What a New Generation Really Thinks About Christianity . . . and Why It Matters* (Grand Rapids, Michigan: Baker Books, 2007).
9. C. S. Lewis, *Mere Christianity* (San Francisco: Harper Collins, 2001), 207.
10. Kanzo Uchimura, *The Complete Works of Kanzo Uchimura, Vol. 1: How I Became a Christian, Out of My Diary* (Tokyo, Japan: Kyobunkwan, 1971), 118.
11. Robert L. Millet, *By Grace Are We Saved* (Salt Lake City: Bookcraft, 1989), 4.
12. Robert L. Millet, "The Perils of Grace," in *BYU Studies Quarterly* 53, no. 2 (2014), 10.
13. David A. Bednar, "In the Strength of the Lord," BYU Devotional Address, 23 October 2001, 3.
14. Henry B. Eyring, *Because He First Loved Us: A Collection of Discourses* (Salt Lake City: Deseret Book, 2002), 38.
15. Jeffrey R. Holland, "Tomorrow the Lord Will Do Wonders among You," *Ensign*, May 2016, 125; emphasis in original.

CHAPTER 2

1. Bruce C. Hafen and Marie K. Hafen, *The Contrite Spirit: How the Temple Helps Us Apply Christ's Atonement* (Salt Lake City: Deseret Book, 2015), 26.
2. Brent J. Schmidt, *Relational Grace: The Reciprocal and Binding Covenant of Charis* (Provo, Utah: BYU Studies, 2015), 19.

NOTES

3. Henry B. Eyring, *Because He First Loved Us: A Collection of Discourses* (Salt Lake City: Deseret Book, 2002), 42.
4. Truman G. Madsen, *The Temple: Where Heaven Meets Earth* (Salt Lake City: Deseret Book, 2008), 69.
5. David A. Bednar, "Bear Up Their Burdens with Ease," *Ensign*, May 2014, 88.
6. See John W. Welch, "The Good Samaritan: Forgotten Symbols," *Ensign*, February 2007, 41–47.
7. Ezra Taft Benson, *Ezra Taft Benson Remembers the Joys of Christmas* (Salt Lake City: Deseret Book, 1988), 11.
8. Bonnie L. Oscarson, "An Exchange of Love between God and Us," in *Between God and Us: How Covenants Connect Us to Heaven* (Salt Lake City: Deseret Book, 2016), 22.

CHAPTER 3

1. See Whitney Laycock, "Finding Christ's Grace throughout the Scriptures," in *BYU Religious Education Student Symposium* (Provo, Utah: Religious Studies Center, Brigham Young University, 2015), 99–108.
2. James E. Faust, "Power of the Priesthood," *Ensign*, May 1997, 41.
3. Richard D. Draper, "Light, Truth, and Grace: Three Themes of Salvation (D&C 93)," in *The Doctrine and Covenants: Sperry Symposium Classics*, ed. Craig K. Manscill (Provo, Utah: Religious Studies Center, Brigham Young University, and Deseret Book, 2004), 243–45.
4. Gordon B. Hinckley, "Excerpts from Recent Addresses of President Gordon B. Hinckley," *Ensign*, August 1998, 72.
5. Joseph Smith, in *The Joseph Smith Papers*, History 1838–1856, vol. E-1, 1 July 1843–30 July 1844, ID #8112, available online at http://www.josephsmithpapers.org, 1971.
6. David A. Bednar, "Always Retain a Remission of Your Sins," *Ensign*, May 2016, 60.
7. Bruce C. Hafen and Marie K. Hafen, *The Contrite Spirit: How the*

Temple Helps Us Apply Christ's Atonement (Salt Lake City: Deseret Book, 2015), 19.

8. See Doctrine and Covenants 66:2; see also Joseph Fielding Smith, *Doctrines of Salvation: Sermons and Writings of Joseph Fielding Smith*, 3 vols., ed. Bruce R. McConkie (Salt Lake City: Deseret Book, 1954–1956), 1:156.
9. Marcus B. Nash, "The New and Everlasting Covenant," *Ensign*, December 2015, 44.
10. Ezra Taft Benson, "A Vision and a Hope for the Youth of Zion," BYU Devotional Address, 12 April 1977, 1.
11. Jeffrey R. Holland, "Abide in Me," *Ensign*, May 2004, 30.
12. See Lois M. Collins, "Studies Explore Religion's Impact on Marriage and Divorce," *Deseret News*, 12 June 2016, 7; see also Dean M. Busby, Jason S. Carroll, and Brian J. Willoughby, "Compatibility or restraint? The effects of sexual timing on marriage relationships," in *Journal of Family Psychology*, vol. 24, no. 6 (December 2010), 766–74.
13. T. Benjamin Spackman, "The Israelite Roots of Atonement Terminology," *BYU Studies Quarterly* 55, no. 1 (2016), 55.
14. Robert L. Millet, *By Grace Are We Saved* (Salt Lake City: Bookcraft, 1989), 101–2.
15. See Doctrine and Covenants 76:54, 59; 93:21–22; see also Hafen and Hafen, *The Contrite Spirit*, 78–91; Camille Fronk Olson, "Covenant Keepers and the Family of God," in *Between God and Us: How Covenants Connect Us to Heaven* (Salt Lake City: Deseret Book, 2016), 124–26.

CHAPTER 4

1. Robert E. Wells, "Adventures of the Spirit," *Ensign*, November 1985, 27.
2. Neal A. Maxwell, "'Apply the Atoning Blood of Christ,'" *Ensign*, November 1997, 24.
3. D. Todd Christofferson, "The Power of Covenants," *Ensign*, May 2009, 22.

NOTES

4. Joseph Fielding Smith, *Answers to Gospel Questions*, 5 vols., comp. Joseph Fielding Smith Jr. (Salt Lake City: Deseret Book, 1957–66), 2:151.
5. Richard G. Scott, "Learning to Recognize Answers to Prayer," *Ensign*, November 1989, 31.
6. Dallin H. Oaks, *With Full Purpose of Heart* (Salt Lake City: Deseret Book, 2002), 169.
7. John H. Groberg, "What Is Your Mission?" BYU Devotional Address, 1 May 1979, 7.
8. Joseph Fielding McConkie and Robert L. Millet, *Joseph Smith: The Choice Seer* (Salt Lake City: Bookcraft, 1996), 75; see also Robert L. Millet, *By Grace Are We Saved* (Salt Lake City: Bookcraft, 1989), 56.
9. See Robert E. Wells, "Adventures of the Spirit," *Ensign*, November 1985, 28.

CHAPTER 5

1. Jeffrey R. Holland, *To My Friends: Messages of Counsel and Comfort* (Salt Lake City: Deseret Book, 2014), 191.
2. Jeffrey R. Holland, "Tomorrow the Lord Will Do Wonders among You," *Ensign*, May 2016, 126; emphasis in original.
3. Taylor Halverson, "How Else Might the Lord's Name Be Taken in Vain?" *Deseret News*, 20 June 2016, http://www.deseretnews.com/article/865656440.
4. John H. Groberg, "The Beauty and Importance of the Sacrament," *Ensign*, May 1989, 38; emphasis added.
5. Henry B. Eyring, *Choose Higher Ground* (Salt Lake City: Deseret Book, 2013), 243.
6. *Addiction Recovery Program: A Guide to Addition Recovery and Healing* (Salt Lake City: LDS Family Services, 2005), 1.
7. Thomas S. Monson, "Choices," *Ensign*, May 2016, 86.
8. Jeffrey R. Holland, "The Justice and Mercy of God," *Ensign*, September 2013, 20; emphasis in original.

NOTES

CHAPTER 6

1. Stephen E. Robinson, "Believing Christ," *Ensign*, April 1992, 8.
2. See Megan Tschannen-Moran, *Trust Matters: Leadership for Successful Schools* (San Francisco: Jossey-Bass, 2014); see also Pam R. Hallam, Hank R. Smith, Julie M. Hite, and Brad Wilcox, "Trust and Collaboration in PLC Teams: Teacher Relationships, Principal Support, and Collaborative Benefits," *NASSP Bulletin* 99, no. 3 (2015), 193–216.
3. Personal notes, 28 April 2016.
4. *Teachings of Presidents of the Church: Lorenzo Snow* (Salt Lake City: The Church of Jesus Christ of Latter-day Saints, 2011), 110.
5. Wendy Ulrich, *Let God Love You: Why We Don't, How We Can* (Salt Lake City: Deseret Book, 2016), 199.
6. Joseph Smith, in *The Joseph Smith Papers*, History 1838–1856, vol. E-1, 1 July 1843–30 July 1844, ID #8112, available online at http://www.josephsmithpapers.org, 1961.
7. Joseph Smith, in *The Joseph Smith Papers*, Discourse, 7 April 1844, as reported by William Clayton, ID #1319, available online at http://www.josephsmithpapers.org, 12.
8. Boyd K. Packer, "Little Children," *Ensign*, November 1986, 17.
9. Joseph Smith, letter to Hyrum Smith with Agnes Coolbrith Smith postscript, 11 April 1839, in *The Joseph Smith Papers*, ID #336, available online at http://www.josephsmithpapers.org.
10. Patricia T. Holland, "Be Renewed in the Spirit of Your Mind," 6 September 1988, unpublished manuscript, used by permission of author.
11. Brigham Young, *Journal of Discourses*, 27 vols., ed. G. D. Watt. (London, England: Latter-day Saints' Book Depot, 1857), 4:54–55.

CHAPTER 7

1. Bo Caldwell, *City of Tranquil Light* (New York: Henry Holt, 2010), 113.

NOTES

2. Neal A. Maxwell, *All These Things Shall Give Thee Experience* (Salt Lake City: Deseret Book, 1979), 101.
3. Bruce C. Hafen, *A Disciple's Life: The Biography of Neal A. Maxwell* (Salt Lake City: Deseret Book, 2002), 20.
4. Neal A. Maxwell, "'Apply the Atoning Blood of Christ,'" *Ensign*, November 1997, 23.
5. Spencer W. Kimball, *Faith Precedes the Miracle* (Salt Lake City: Deseret Book, 1972), 97.
6. David A. Bednar, "Learning to Love Learning," BYU Commencement Address, 24 April 2008, 2.
7. Chieko N. Okazaki, *Lighten Up!* (Salt Lake City: Deseret Book, 1993), 174.
8. See Friedrich Nietzsche, *Twilight of the Idols or How to Philosophize with a Hammer*, trans. Daniel Fidel Ferrer; Public Domain: https://archive.org.
9. Richard G. Scott, "Personal Strength through the Atonement of Jesus Christ," *Ensign*, November 2013, 84.

CHAPTER 8

1. Brigham Young, *The Complete Discourses of Brigham Young*, 5 vols., ed. Richard S. Van Wagoner (Salt Lake City: Smith-Pettit Foundation, 2009), 1:276.
2. Bruce R. McConkie, "What Think Ye of Salvation by Grace?" BYU Devotional Address, 10 January 1984, 4.
3. Gene R. Cook, "The Grace of the Lord," *Ensign*, May 1993, 80.
4. Gerald N. Lund, "Salvation: By Grace or Works?" *Ensign*, April 1981, 23; emphasis in original.
5. M. Russell Ballard, "Building Bridges of Understanding," *Ensign*, June 1998, 65.
6. See Colleen McDannel and Bernhard Lang, *Heaven: A History* (New Haven, Connecticut: Yale University Press, 1988).
7. Dallin H. Oaks, "Have You Been Saved?" *Ensign*, May 1998, 55.

NOTES

8. Barnard N. Madsen, *The Truman G. Madsen Story: A Life of Study and Faith* (Salt Lake City: Deseret Book, 2016), 479.
9. Joseph Smith, in *The Joseph Smith Papers*, Discourse, 5 January 1841, as reported by unknown scribe A, ID #7837, available online at http://www.josephsmithpapers.org, 1.
10. Joseph Smith, in *The Joseph Smith Papers*, History 1838–1856, vol. D-1, 1 August 1842–1 July 1843, ID #7624, available online at http://www.josephsmithpapers.org, 1549.
11. D. Todd Christofferson, "Free Forever, to Act for Themselves," *Ensign*, November 2014, 18.
12. See Thomas S. Monson, "Choices," *Ensign*, May 2016, 86.
13. Tad R. Callister, "Repentance: The Pathway to Perfection," in *Between God and Us: How Covenants Connect Us to Heaven* (Salt Lake City: Deseret Book, 2016), 89.
14. See James R. Clark, comp., *Messages of the First Presidency* (Salt Lake City: Bookcraft, 1971), 5:4.
15. Lucile C. Tate, *David B. Haight: The Life Story of a Disciple* (Salt Lake City: Bookcraft, 1987), 130.
16. Karen Lynn Davidson, David J. Whittaker, Mark Ashurst-McGee, and Richard L. Jensen, eds., *The Joseph Smith Papers, Histories, Volume 1: Joseph Smith Histories, 1832–1844* (Salt Lake City: The Church Historian's Press, 2012), 402–4.
17. Joseph Smith, in *The Joseph Smith Papers*, History 1838–1856, vol. C-1, 2 November 1838–31 July 1842, ID #7513, available online at http://www.josephsmithpapers.org, 8.
18. Bruce R. McConkie, *The Promised Messiah: The First Coming of Christ* (Salt Lake City, Deseret Book, 1981), 347.

CHAPTER 9

1. Bruce C. Hafen, "The Value of the Veil," *Ensign*, June 1977, 13; emphasis in original.
2. Dallin H. Oaks, "Have You Been Saved?" *Ensign*, May 1998, 57.

NOTES

3. D. Todd Christofferson, "The Power of Covenants," *Ensign*, May 2009, 22.
4. Robin Scott Jensen, Richard E. Turley Jr., and Riley M. Lorimer, eds., *The Joseph Smith Papers, Revelations and Translations, Volume 2: Published Revelations* (Salt Lake City: The Church Historian's Press, 2011), 364.
5. T. Benjamin Spackman, "The Israelite Roots of Atonement Terminology," *BYU Studies Quarterly* 55, no. 1 (2016), 53.
6. Andrew C. Skinner, "The Nature and Character of God," BYU Devotional Address, 11 April 2006, 2.
7. Clark B. Hinckley, *Christopher Columbus: A Man among the Gentiles* (Salt Lake City: Deseret Book, 2014), 213.
8. Thornton Wilder, *Our Town* (New York: Harper and Row, 1957), act 3, 100.
9. See Andrew C. Skinner, *To Become Like God: Witnesses of Our Divine Potential* (Salt Lake City: Deseret Book, 2016).
10. See William Shakespeare, *Hamlet*, act 2, scene 2, lines 300–305 (Oxford, England: Clarendon Press, 1987).
11. See Robert Browning, *Rabbi Ben Ezra* (New York: Thomas Y. Crowell, 1902), 31.
12. Tad R. Callister, "Our Identity and Our Destiny," BYU Devotional Address, 14 August 2012, 9.
13. Joseph Smith, in *The Joseph Smith Papers*, History 1838–1856, vol. C-1, Addenda, ID #8119, available online at http://www.josephsmithpapers.org, 62.
14. Bruce C. Hafen and Marie K. Hafen, *The Contrite Spirit: How the Temple Helps Us Apply Christ's Atonement* (Salt Lake City: Deseret Book, 2015), 8; emphasis in original.
15. A. LeGrand Richards, *Called to Teach: The Legacy of Karl G. Maeser* (Salt Lake City: Religious Studies Center, Brigham Young University, and Deseret Book, 2014), xxxi.
16. See Dieter F. Uchtdorf, "The Gift of Grace," *Ensign*, May 2015, 108.
17. D. Todd Christofferson, "Free Forever, to Act for Themselves," *Ensign*, November 2014, 17.

18. Bruce R. McConkie, *Doctrinal New Testament Commentary* 3 vols., (Salt Lake City: Bookcraft, 1965–1973), 2:422.

CHAPTER 10

1. Dale G. Renlund, "'That I Might Draw All Men unto Me,'" *Ensign*, May 2016, 40.
2. Ibid., 41.
3. Cheryl Harward Wilcox, "Melva's Last Supper," *Ensign*, October 2016, 11.
4. Lucile C. Tate, *David B. Haight: The Life Story of a Disciple* (Salt Lake City: Bookcraft, 1987), 322.

INDEX

Acceptance, 17–19
Adam and Eve, 147–48, 172
Addiction. *See* Bondage
Adventures of the Spirit, 66–67, 87–88
Agency, 62
Alma, 28, 146, 165
Anderson, Scott, 149
Appearances, 177–79
Atonement: grace and, 10; Jesus Christ as only one authorized for, 20–21; and need-based help, 37–38; applying, 67; mocking, 104, 110; healing through, 108; greatness of, 173–76; transformation through, 179–80

Ballard, M. Russell, 145–46
Baptism, 157–58
Bednar, David A., 34–35
Benevolence, 115, 116–17
Benson, Ezra Taft, 41
Blessing, for wounded shoulder, 188
Blessings, of sacrifice, 53–55
Bodies, 148–51
Bondage, 89–91; enduring and, 91–93; and taking Lord's name in vain, 93–96; reaching out for help in, 96–99; keeping long-term perspective through, 99–102; healing and, 102–12
Books, 45–47
Brain tumor, student diagnosed with, 126–28, 133–38, 140–41
Branch, relationship with Christ compared to vine and, 32–34
Bridegroom and bride, covenant relationship compared to, 39–41
Bullying, 154–55, 160–61

Caldwell, Bo, 129–30
"Called to Serve," 142
Calling birds, 6–7
Callister, Tad R., 154, 172–73
Canals, Omar, 186
Captain Moroni, 86–87
Carter, Corrina, 78
Cause for Hope Foundation, 192–96
Celestial souls, 181–85
Change: through grace, 1–2, 17–19,

INDEX

181–85; need and power to, 21–22. *See also* Transformation
Change of heart, 110, 174
Chastity, 57–59
Chick, hatching of, 100
Child(ren): understanding of, of love, 26; relationship with Christ compared to nurturing adult and, 28–32
Chile, acts of service in, 51–53
Christmas, 183–84
Christofferson, D. Todd, 8–9, 72, 152, 167
Cochran, Joe, 87
Colly birds, 6–7
Columbus, Christopher, 170
"Come Thou Fount of Every Blessing," 44–45
Comfort, through Holy Ghost, 76–78
Commandments, 55–57
Companions yoked together, 34–36
Competence: as facet of trust, 115; of God, 118–19
Confession, 98
Consecration, 59–61
Cook, Gene R., 145
Corianton, 87
Covenant relationship: grace as, 26–28, 41–43; compared to that of nurturing adult and child, 28–32; compared to vine and branch, 32–34; compared to companions yoked together, 34–36; compared to good Samaritan and injured traveler, 36–38; compared to bridegroom and bride, 39–41
Covenants: and receiving grace, 49; spiritual adoption through, 63–64

Dalton, Elaine S., 60
Dead, ordinances for, 16–17, 163
Death, 77–78, 147–51
Debt, 44–45
Dessert plates, 6–7
Dew, Sheri, 10
Divine kinship, 170
Draper, Richard D., 48
Dream homes, 181

Edmunds, Mary Ellen, 149
Education, 85–86
Endowment, 50
Enduring, 91–93
Ensign Peak, 139–40
Eternal life, 166–67
Eve, 147–48, 172
Exaltation, 166–70
Eyring, Henry B., 19–20, 28, 98

Faith, through trials, 140–41
Fall of Adam and Eve, 147–48, 172
Families, sealing of, 16–17
Family relations, 175–76
Father, God as, 169–70
Fault-finding, 119–22
Fillmore, Brent, 33–34, 54
First Vision, 144–45
Flaws, 12, 119–22
Forgiveness, 109–11
Forsaking, 103–4, 110

Gates of heaven, 180–81
Gifford, Dan, 192, 195
Gift, grace as, 27
Gift of tongues, 177
Goals, setting, 98
God: covenant relationship with, 26–43; indebtedness to, 44–45; power of, 47–48; sealing to, 62–65; Holy Ghost as witness of, 74–76; eternal perspective of, 99; trusting, 114, 115–22; timing of, 118; character of, 122–25, 128–32; becoming like,

INDEX

167–70; as Father, 169–70; being in presence of, 174–75; becoming one with, 176–80

Godhead, 11. *See also* God; Holy Ghost; Jesus Christ

Golding, Julia, 29–32

Gonzales, Fernando, 78–80

Good Samaritan, 36–38

Gordon, Grace, 142

Gospel: living, 55–57; internalizing, 177–79

Grace: change through, 1–2, 17–19, 181–85; receiving, 2–3; understanding, 4–5, 7; meaning of, 7–12; perils of, 13–16; and truth, 24–25; as covenant relationship, 26–28, 41–43; indebtedness for, 44–45; levels of, 45–48; Holy Ghost as messenger of, 67–71; "saved by grace," 143–46; giving, to others, 191–97. *See also* Receiving grace

Grace for grace, 191–97

Gracias, 186

Gratitude, 186–88

Groberg, John H., 82, 94–95

Guidance, through Holy Ghost, 78–82

Gwyther, Louisa, 22–24

Hafen, Bruce C., 27, 166, 176

Hafen, Marie K., 27, 176

Haight, David B., 158–59, 196

Halfway house, author speaks to women from, 95–96

Halverson, Taylor, 94

Harward, Melva, 189–91

Healing, 102–12

Heart, change of, 110, 174

Heaven: gates and windows of, 180–81; being prepared for, 181–85

Hell, 163–65

Help, reaching out for, 96–99

Herod, 184

Hewitt, Eliza ("Lidie"), 138–39

Hill, Sarah, 152–53

Hinckley, Clark B., 170

Holland, Jeffrey R., 20, 51, 93, 107

Holland, Patricia T., 123–24

Holy Ghost: grace from, 11; adventures of, 66–67, 87–88; as messenger of grace, 67–71; roles of, 71; recognizing, 71–73; as witness of Father and Son, 74–76; as comforter, 76–78; as guide, 78–82; as sanctifier, 82–87; gift of, 158

Honesty, 115, 117

Hughes, Kathleen H., 116

Ignorance, 107, 159–63

Immortality, 166

Inadequacies, 12

Indebtedness, 44–45

"I Stand All Amazed," 2–3

Jesus Christ: grace from, 11; merits, mercy, and grace of, 20–21, 24; grace and truth of, 24–25; covenant relationship with, 26–43; spiritual progression of, 48; receiving, 61; becoming like, 62; why we believe in, 69; Holy Ghost as witness of, 74–76; taking name of, in vain, 93–96; trusting, 119; strength through, 135–38; repentance made possible through, 151–56; spiritual rebirth through, 156–59; being in presence of, 175; mission of, 184; remembering, 189–91. *See also* Atonement

Jones, Barbara, 84

Jones, Hal, 84–86, 131

Kimball, Spencer W., 132

INDEX

Kinship, divine, 170
Kirtland Temple, 11–12

Lamanites, 89
Laycock, Landon, 184
Laycock, Larry, 184
Les Misérables (Hugo), 192
Lewis, C. S., 13
Light of Christ, 157
Limhi, people of, 89–90, 93, 103
Long-term perspective, 99–102
Love, 26, 128–32
Lund, Gerald N., 145

Madsen, Truman, 28, 150
Maeser, Karl G., 179
Marriage: covenant relationship compared to, 39–41; and blessings of sacrifice, 53–54; and healing from past, 102–12
Maxwell, Neal A., 67, 130–31
McConkie, Bruce R., 145, 165, 183
McNary, Brad, 1–2
McNary, Rachel, 1, 2
Meekness, 35–36
Mercy, 20–21, 24
Merits, of Jesus Christ, 20–21, 24
Millet, Robert L., 15, 64
Miracles, 111, 177
Mission, sense of, 170–73
Missionary/Missionaries: clothing for, 51–52; receives answer to question, 69–71; teach professor, 83; advised to keep long-term perspective, 101–2; undergoes change, 174–75
Mistrust, sources of, 116–19
Monson, Thomas S., 106
Moroni, 86–87
Mortality, 132–33, 176
Moses, 18–19
Mount Zion, saviors on, 191–92

Name, changing, 39–41
Nash, Marcus B., 50
Need, help based on, 37–38
Nephi, 124–25
Nephites, 89–90
New and everlasting covenant, 50
New Testament Church, 143–44
Nielsen, Kayci, 173
Nurturing adult, relationship with Christ compared to child and, 28–32

Oaks, Dallin H., 81, 147, 166–67
Obedience, 51–55
Okazaki, Chieko, 135
Olson, Camille Fronk, 4
Open gates and windows, 180–81
Openness: as facet of trust, 115; of God, 117–18
Ordinances, 13, 16–17, 49–50, 163
Outer darkness, 164
Oxen, 34–36

Packer, Boyd K., 123
Parable of talents, 46–47
Passions, bridling, 58–59
Past, healing from, 102–12
Paul, 170–71
Perego, Ugo A., 67, 68
Perfection, 92–93, 153, 154, 182
Perfectionism, 15, 119–22
Perry, Janice Kapp, 59–60
Perry, Steven Kapp, 32–33
Personal revelation, 78–82
Perspective, keeping long-term, 99–102
Pilot, service rendered by, 51–52
Pioneers, 139–40
Plan of salvation, 132–33
Pledge of Allegiance, 179
Pornography, 97, 102–12
Power of God, 47–48, 128–32

INDEX

Power of godliness, 72, 167–68
Prayer, answers to, 117–18
Premortal world, 119, 149
Priesthood, 10–11, 134
Priesthood blessing, for wounded shoulder, 188
Professor, experiences change of heart, 82–84
"Proffers," 3
Progress: spiritual, 8–9, 10, 12, 176; through grace, 19–20; through enduring, 91–92

Quicksand, 96–97

Rane, Walter, 2
Reaching out, for help, 96–99
Rebirth, spiritual, 156–59
Receiving grace, 44–45; and levels of grace, 45–48; and spiritual progression, 48–51; through obedience and sacrifice, 51–55; through living gospel, 55–57; through chastity, 57–59; through consecration, 59–61; through sealings, 62–65
Reconciliation, 183
Relationship. See Covenant relationship
Reliability: as facet of trust, 115; of God, 118
Renlund, Dale G., 187, 189
Repentance, 103–4, 151–56
Restoration, 4, 144–45
Resurrection, 147, 149, 150–51
Revelation, 78–82
Rich, Brent, 127, 135
Rich, Lori, 135
Robinson, Robert, 44–45, 65
Robinson, Stephen E., 113–14
Rome, Italy, talk for fireside at, 67–71

Rostedt, Leanne, 133–34, 140–41
Rostedt, Tyler, 126–28, 133–38, 140–41
Rules, 55–57

Sacrament, 3, 94–96, 189–91, 197
Sacrifice, 51–55
Salvation: through grace, 143–46, 164–65; kinds of, 146–47; from death, 147–51; from sin, 151–56; from our worst selves, 156–59; from ignorance, 159–63; from hell, 163–65. See also Exaltation
Sanctification, 82–87
Sanders, Brett, 187
Santiago Chile Temple, 74–75
Satan, 57, 62, 105, 149, 151, 164
Saul, 170–71
Saviors on Mount Zion, 191–92
Schmidt, Brent J., 27, 42
Scott, Richard G., 81, 137
Sealing, 16–17, 62–65
Self-criticism, 119–22
Self-esteem, 160–61
Self-improvement, 19–20
Self-reliance, 192–95
Sense of mission, 170–73
Service, 41, 43, 51–53, 83
Shoulder, blessing for wounded, 187–88
Sin: confessing, 98; and salvation by grace, 144; repentance and, 151–56
Single mother, 55–56
Skinner, Andrew C., 170
Slavery. See Bondage
Smith, Joseph, 49, 122, 130, 150–51, 162–63, 174
Smith, Joseph Fielding, 75–76
Smoking, 95–96
Snow, Lorenzo, 119
Spirit. See Holy Ghost

INDEX

Spiritual adoption, 63–65
Spiritual progression, 8–9, 10, 12, 48–51, 91–92, 176
Spiritual rebirth, 156–59
Spirit world, 163–64
Stalactites and stalagmites, 33–34
Strength: gaining, 100–101; through Jesus Christ, 135–38
Suffering. *See* Trials
Support system, building, 96–99
"Sweet Hour of Prayer," 15
Swimming lessons, 113–14

Talents, parable of, 46–47
Talk, changed by author following prompting, 67–71
Taylor, George, 22–23
Taylor, Louisa Gwyther, 22–24
Temple clothes, 52
Temptation, ridding ourselves of, 97–99
Ten Commandments, 18–19
Tender mercies, 9–10
"There Is Sunshine in My Soul Today," 138–39
Tolerance, 17–19
Tongues, gift of, 177
Transformation, 176–80; and becoming like God, 167–70; and sense of mission, 170–73; and greatness of Atonement, 173–76; through at-one-ment, 176–80; purpose of, 180–85. *See also* Change
Trials: and character of God, 128–32; learning from, 132–34; happiness through, 138–39; as monuments of grace, 139–40; faith through, 140–41
True doctrine, 122–25
"True Vine, The," 32–33

Trust, 113–15; facets of, 115–16; and sources of mistrust, 116–19; relearning, 119–22
Truth, 24–25
"Twelve Days of Christmas" dessert plates, 6–7

Uchimura, Kanzo, 13–14
Uchtdorf, Dieter F., 8, 10, 180
Ulrich, Wendy, 122
Upward pull, 16–20

Vain, 94
Valjean, 192
Vine and branch, relationship with Christ compared to, 32–34
Violin, 51

Weaknesses, 12. *See also* Flaws
Welch, John W., 36
Wells, Helen, 88
Wells, Robert E., 66, 87–88
"We Thank Thee, O God, for a Prophet," 92
Wilcox, Cheryl Harward, 189–91
Wilcox, David, 101–2
Wilcox, Ray T., 77–78
Wilcox, Russell, 9, 16, 26, 187–88
Wilcox, Trish, 9
Wilcox, Wendee, 165, 181
Wilder, Thornton, 171–72
Windows of heaven, 180–81
Wise men, 184
Works, 8–9, 14–15, 145–46, 186
Worthiness, 92–93, 94–95

Yellow lights, 80–82
Yoke, 34–36
Young, Brigham, 124, 139, 145

Zeezrom, 146, 165